Victory
Over
Schizophrenia

Also by Paul Penman:

Published Works
The God of a Second Chance (National Library of Australia)
Why Did Grandpa Go to Africa? (Zaccmedia UK)
The Wiluna Wangka, 3 volumes (State Library of Western Australia)

Private Collection
The Penman Family
A History of the Oakleigh Christian Centre
The King's Jubilee Award
A Civilized Form of Hand-to-Hand Combat
'Parnie': William Dulling McCombie
The Mission in Wiluna
Thelma: The Girlie from Caragabal
Parson Penman: A Power in the Pulpit
Seven Years in the Valley
Love Never Fails

Occasional Articles
Hobnobbing with Writing Royalty
I've Been to Jail!
I'll Be a Good Girl, Daddy, If You Let Me Sing
Knitting as Occupational Therapy
(Broadcast on ABC National Radio)

The Wickedness of Evil Spirits
Time
Scintillating Sydney
Say It with Flowers
The Girl in the Band
It Was the Perfect Time for a Farm Holiday
Puppy Love
Frivolity
The Accident
The Strange Package outside My Door
A Bath. Oh! ... What Bliss!
My Love of Music
The Journey from Head to Heart

Victory
Over
Schizophrenia

My Journey with Peter

A Memoir

Paul Penman

Published by Zaccmedia
www.zaccmedia.com
info@zaccmedia.com

Published November 2016

ISBN: 978-1-911211-43-3

British Library Cataloguing-in-Publication Data
A catalogue record for this book is available from the British Library

Definition of schizophrenia

Any of various psychotic disorders characterised by
a breakdown of integrated personality functioning,
withdrawal from reality, emotional blunting and
distortion, and disturbances in thought and behaviour.

The Macquarie Dictionary

Origin of the definition of schizophrenia

The word 'schizophrenia' has been ascribed to the Swiss
psychiatrist and psychologist (Paul) Eugen Bleuler
(1857–1939) who coined the word in 1908. The word
describes the disorder previously known as *dementia
praecox*, from the Latin meaning 'prematurely out of
one's mind', the name given by Emil Kraepelin, and for
his study of schizophrenics. Bleuler tended to oppose the
view that schizophrenia is caused by irreversible brain
damage, but did not believe in the possibility of healing.
Bleuler emphasised the associative disturbances, not the
demons.

Wikipedia

'Am I my brother's keeper?'

Genesis 4:9

In loving memory:

Thelma Mary (McCombie) Penman
(1905–1977)

John Leslie Penman
(1910–1990)

Peter John McCombie Penman
(1941–2013)

CONTENTS

Peter

Saint Peter

Now I think there is a likeness
'Twixt St Peter's life and mine,
For he did a lot of trampin'
Long ago in Palestine.
He was 'union' when the workers
First began to organise
And – I'm glad that old St Peter
Keeps the gate of Paradise.

Henry Lawson (1867–1922), the Bard of Australia
'Verses Popular and Humorous', *A Camp-Fire Yarn: Complete Works
1885–1900*, verse 1 (p 275)

ABOUT THE AUTHOR

Paul taken at Manly Golf Club, School Reunion,
2009

Paul Leslie McCombie Penman was born in Manly, a seaside
suburb of Sydney, and was educated at Manly (Village) Public
School and Manly Boys' High School. He spent twenty-five years
in the advertising profession in Australia and briefly in South
Africa. His career began in advertising agencies where he special-
ised in media buying. He then moved into the media itself with
Rupert Murdoch's (Sydney) *Sunday Telegraph* where he became
their top space salesman. He also worked with the Packers and
the Fairfax family, including for *The Age* in Melbourne. Paul is a
Fellow of the Advertising Institute of Australia and also qualified
with Tennis Australia as an Advanced Coach. In academia he has

earned degrees as a Bachelor of Arts in Intercultural Studies and Bachelor of Social Science (Honours); he also holds a Graduate Diploma of Arts (Writing). In 2013 Paul withdrew from the degree of Doctor of Philosophy (Theology) at the University of Newcastle where he was documenting the life of his great-grandfather, the Reverend John Penman, who made a significant contribution to the Australasian Methodist Church in the colonial era and at federation.

His book *Why Did Grandpa Go to Africa?*, published in 2014, draws a graphic picture of his exploits as a missionary in Nelson Mandela's 'New South Africa' and has been widely acclaimed. *Victory Over Schizophrenia: My Journey with Peter* shows a deep understanding of this complex mental disorder.

Paul has two married daughters and four grandchildren and now resides in marvellous Melbourne.

With a cheeky grin he says, 'I'd prefer to wear out than rust.' Paul is certainly a bundle of energy and lives life to the full.

PREFACE

This book is about my journey with Peter, my older brother and only sibling, who was diagnosed with schizophrenia and depression in his early twenties. The condition became chronic. Many years later he developed frontal lobe dementia,* and shortly before he died in 2013 an inoperable growth was discovered. Peter had a heart attack and died as a result. He was seventy-two.

On our mother's deathbed in 1977 she whispered to me, '*Who will look after Peter?*'

Instinctively I knew this was to be my role, and at great emotional cost I honoured our mother's final request until Peter's dying day. Now that he has passed on, I'm fulfilling her heartfelt plea by sharing Peter's story from my perspective.

For over thirty years I became Peter's unofficial carer and journeyed with him not only emotionally but physically and spiritually* through New South Wales, Queensland and as far afield as Nhulunbuy in the Northern Territory. I lived in Peter's dilapidated caravan for six months while he was incarcerated in the psychiatric unit of a regional hospital. Unless you've had this or similar experiences you won't imagine the debasement and pain of such experiences for Peter and for me.

For the entire period of Peter's long journey into madness he lived in a number of caravan parks, rooming houses, halfway houses, aged-care facilities and finally in nursing homes. This was interspersed with short stays in general hospitals and long stays in psychiatric institutions where electroconvulsive therapy* was administered and at one point I had to give permission for him to be administered 'the drug of last resort'. There were the attempted suicides. Those of you reading this who've survived such situations will appreciate the dilemma of family and the concern of nursing staff, general practitioners, clinical psychologists and consultant psychiatrists. Throughout this journey Peter had no option but to play the role of a willing patient and I had to stand by, looking on, knowing all the time these medical interventions hadn't got to the root of the problem.

Peter's plight was so untenable that years ago I prayed that God would take him Home. As a born-again Christian,* Peter knew that to go Home meant to spend Eternity with God. But God didn't answer my desperate prayers, until later I discovered I wasn't praying in accordance with His perfect will. God knew I wanted to get my brother back, the 'big brother' of our childhood, but He had a much better plan and His timing is always perfect and His ways turned out to be much higher than mine. In desperation one day I called out to God – and everything was to change dramatically.

'Lord,* what is to become of Peter? For these past thirty years I've honoured our mother's dying wish and look at Peter now. Why have You allowed him to suffer?' (You can hear how angry I'd become with God!)

The Lord then spoke into my spirit, not in an audible way but I knew it was the voice of God: '*You have honoured your mother's dying wish. Now it's time for you to seek prayer counselling for Peter.*'

I sought intercessory* prayer counselling immediately, and in God's perfect timing I saw a miracle.

An enormous debt of gratitude is owed to the many people who travelled with me on this research and writing journey. By not naming them I've respected their privacy. They all know who they are. They stuck with me through thick and thin, encouraging me and sometimes chastising me but loving me throughout the process. I was simply the penman. All honour and glory belongs to the Lord.

---

* Terms marked with an asterisk throughout the book are explained in the Glossary.

INTRODUCTION

From the outset you must understand that I have no formal qualifications to write on such a complex subject as schizophrenia. My academic qualifications are in theology, social science, advertising, sport and writing, but what I do bring to the table is years of hands-on experience. This anecdotal evidence as an unofficial carer (not only for my brother but for our mother before him) is qualification enough. In addition, my own life experiences have qualified me through my tough apprenticeship in the School of Hard Knocks and at the University of the Street. Compared with today's 60 million refugees and survivors of the Holocaust, my life's journey has been a Sunday School picnic, but sadly it wasn't the same for Peter. His life potential was never achieved and the dreams, visions and all the desires of his heart were never fulfilled.

Because Peter was a humble and self-effacing man I doubt he would have ever wanted anything documented about him after he died. Indeed, one of my daughters said so and at the time I agreed, but as time passed I recognised that to record Peter's journey could help those living with the curse of schizophrenia. For me it would act as a healing balm from sad and deeply entrenched memories.

In the eyes of many reading this, the methodology in the processing of this book will be unconventional. The first thing I did was to wait on God.* It seemed a good idea to put pen to paper a long time ago but the timing had to be right. After Peter's sudden death I grieved for months and so profound was that grief my family was quite concerned about my mental health. Fortunately I took their advice and was given excellent insight by an experienced clinical psychologist. I prayed constantly and by June 2015 it was time to begin the research. Take a glance at the Bibliography and you'll see that few research options remain unturned. I delved into books, magazines, newspaper articles, medical literature and journals, search engines, websites and YouTube. This thorough research spanned nearly twelve months, and throughout this process and during the writing everything was undergirded with prayer.

When the mass media in Australia was recently awash with the sexual abuse scandals inside and outside the Church, in particular the inquiry implicating the former Roman Catholic Archbishop George Pell, now ensconced in the Vatican in Rome, and more recently the cover-up in the Anglican Church in Newcastle, a mate of mine asked me if my brother had ever been sexually abused. I was shocked at this question – the thought had never entered my head. So I pondered his question and decided to ask the Lord in prayer. As I'm a born-again believer and was baptised in the Holy Spirit* many years ago and I've been on missionary journeys to Africa,[1] to an Aboriginal community in remote

Western Australia[2] and on many other Christian missions, I felt fully qualified to pray in the hope of gaining some insight. So I prayed, 'Dearest Heavenly Father, You've heard this question. Was Peter ever sexually abused?'

In silence I waited for the Lord's reply, and through a word of knowledge* it soon came: '*I have heard your prayer. Yes, Peter was sexually abused.*'

I was shown a clear picture of his Scout master, the perpetrator of this crime. The Scout master's face was familiar to me – a man in his twenties who'd worked as an usher at the Metro picture theatre opposite the beach in Manly where we lived as children. Peter was thirteen years old.

'*You are to write a book about schizophrenia, emphasising sexual abuse as the root of this psychosis.**'

Beloved reader, you've *no* idea how I've agonised over including this revelation. Peter may have put this incident clear out of his mind, never connecting it with his later diagnosis of chronic schizophrenia. I also wrestled about revealing that I had also been sexually abused as a baby, so I initially deleted all reference to any sexual abuse. But for weeks afterwards I was ill at ease so I blocked it all out of my head; instead I started writing short articles about my own life that I believed would ultimately become chapters in an autobiography. But when this writing detour ended I still couldn't rest. Should I tell the world at large that Peter and I were sexually abused? So as I usually do, I waited in prayer for confirmation to come in one way or another.

It was the Lenten season, the forty days observed by Christians throughout the world before the Passion of Christ.* During this season many Christians fast* and I wondered what I was to go without. It soon became obvious: I was to neither watch television nor drink alcohol.

'God... what are You trying to tell me?'

Then one morning the word of the Lord came to me through the Scriptures* in Psalm 126:5: 'Those who sow with tears will reap with songs of joy.' In tears I got out of bed immediately, interpreting this to mean I must include the revelation of not only Peter's abuse but also my own. This disclosure would act as the balm of Gilead* for so many readers who have also been sexually abused. *What followed then is extraordinary!*

The Sunday after I'd prayed and received the answer, I was having coffee after our regular Healing Service* at my charismatic* Anglican church, St Paul's in North Caulfield, a Melbourne suburb. A middle-aged woman, whom I'd observed earlier but had never met, came and sat next to me and we exchanged the usual pleasantries. Then suddenly and inexplicably she confided, 'You know, Paul, I was sexually abused as a child.'

What is so extraordinary is the fact that the Holy Spirit* revealed to me that this woman had been sexually abused as soon as she began to walk towards me! Similar scenarios were to be played out for weeks afterwards when a number of women revealed their innermost secrets about having been sexually abused. Remarkably I was soon to observe people who'd been sexually abused but had no conscious knowledge of the abuse themselves! They'd blocked it out – their tongues had been muted as mine was when I was sexually abused all those years ago. Many of these innocent victims were taking prescribed drugs for schizophrenia, but the root, their sexual abuse, had neither been revealed to them nor to their family, consultant psychiatrists, psychologists or even to members of the Healing Team* here at St Paul's.

Some readers will say that what I've just disclosed is fanciful, outrageous or even absurd, but that's not the case. I encourage the incredulous reader to undertake your own research and navigate the vast literature available or use your search engines;[3] then you'll discover that each and every one of your concerns will be dispelled. What I've written here is true, testable and irrefutable.

Because of the way my prayer was answered I've focused on schizophrenia as a consequence of sexual abuse. Because of the trauma and misplaced guilt associated with the original event, many or most victims may have blocked out the first incident. I've kept away from the diagnosis of schizophrenia as a result of the ingestion of illegal drugs, although it is certainly possible that the root cause of the drug addiction could have been the original sexual abuse.

1 *Why Did Grandpa Go to Africa?* is available at Amazon, Book Depository etc. Also at Readings, Koorong, and your local library.
2 I spent a year in Wiluna, a remote mining town on the edge of the Little Sandy Desert in Western Australia and produced a newspaper, *The Wiluna Wangka.*
3 At the back of this book I've provided a list of most of the resources I've consulted.

PART ONE

CHAPTER 1

IN THE BEGINNING

Peter and Paul

Peter John McCombie Penman, or Peter Boy as he was affectionately known as a toddler, was named after Peter in the Bible. Also named after Bible characters were our father John and his grandfather the Reverend John Penman.[1] Our name Penman originated in Scotland at Fifeshire near Edinburgh.

McCombie is our mother's maiden name, her family also originating in Scotland. When I was researching the family history at the Bodleian Library in Oxford some years ago, I dug down deep to unearth a few family skeletons. There were men of the cloth, the occasional scribe and of course the alcoholics. Allow me to stretch a long bow by saying that the Penmans were scribes/secretaries in the royal court of Mary, Queen of Scots. It would be stretching an even longer bow to say that an ancestor of our mother, Thelma Mary, was a courtier in Queen Mary's court. Writers call this poetic licence!

Peter was born in Sydney's Waverley War Memorial Hospital on 23 January 1941. Dad was a teller with the Bank of New South Wales in the eastern suburbs and Mum was confined to home duties in Maroubra. Dad was transferred in 1942 to the Manly branch on the Corso[2] where Westpac still stands.

I entered the world on 7 July 1942 at the Wyuna Private Hospital in Little Manly. The Western world was at war when Peter and I were born as it was in the middle of the Second World War and our flat overlooking Sydney harbour was in the sights of midget submarines sent from our faraway enemy Japan.

Peter and I were in the same class at kindergarten in Gilbert Park overlooking the Manly Oval, Manly Village and the Pacific Ocean. Here I was to have my first vivid memory of Peter as my big brother, my protector and my hero. It's all rather embarrassing really! One day I had an accident in the playground – yes, I'd pooped my pants – and Peter came to the rescue and cleaned up the mess. Would big brothers do that today?

We attended Sunday School at St Matthew's Church of England,[3] also on the Corso. In those days Sunday School was held in the afternoon and Mum and Dad would always be keenly waiting for us afterwards, sitting lovingly on a park bench overlooking the harbour. These Sundays were idyllic.

Peter and Paul

Our rented flat was tiny compared with home units, apartments and condominiums today. Before going to sleep at night Peter and I would sometimes hold hands across our single beds, pretending a train was coming with our hands acting as a barrier. One of us would then 'toot', a signal for the boom gate to close. These are fond memories of innocent, trusting, happy and carefree days.

Like Dad, Peter grew to be strong, athletic and handsome in spite of the fact that when he was eight he contracted scarlet fever and whooping cough; after being confined for six weeks inside the Quarantine Station at North Head (now renamed Q Station), fortunately he returned home fit and feisty. Mum was known as Penny by her golfing associates and was tall, refined and carried herself with dignity. Peter joined the Cubs and later the Scouts and later played junior football for Manly. He became a strong swimmer after lessons at the Manly Baths and later joined the

Mum and Dad

Manly Surf Life-Saving Club where he gained his Bronze Medallion. Mum introduced Peter to that royal and ancient Scottish game known as golf which he took to like a fish to water.

We both had an aversion to school as did many who lived in Manly, the original surfer's paradise. On school days we would have much preferred to go surfing or to swim in the harbour pools than to sit in a stuffy classroom, especially during Sydney's long, hot summers, but we had no option. Peter survived primary school and then went to Balgowlah Technical School over the road from the golf club where Mum had become their Associate Ladies' Captain and later Associate Club Champion. After successfully completing the Intermediate Certificate at what was then known as 'shack town' because of the removable classrooms, Peter left to begin an apprenticeship as a carpenter.

In the 1950s, surf clubs in Australia could lure a young, virile, testosterone-charged young man into lots of trouble with the

4

opposite sex. Fortunately for Peter, Mum and Dad saw the writing on the wall so had steered Peter into golf as occupational therapy! He joined the prestigious Manly Golf Club where he played with gusto, and in time represented them in Junior (Under 23) competition.

The Christmas school holidays were spent idyllically either on Grandfather's farm, Carinya, or at Grandpop's holiday house, Araluen, by the lakes and near the sea. We were both so blessed to have grandfathers as Dad's mother died when we were quite young and Mum's mother died in tragic circumstances in a mental asylum when Mum was only eighteen.

At Carinya, Mum's father's 40-acre property at Horsley Park on the outskirts of Sydney, we rode horses, milked the cow, collected hen's eggs, swam in the dam, and in the evenings Parnie (as we lovingly called our grandfather) taught us to play board games, especially draughts. During the day we often played havoc in the

huge orchard and frequently went amok when our carers were out of sight. Here in semi-rural Australia we could roam free, escaping the confines of life in suburbia.

Grandpop's holiday house, north of Gosford on the central coast at Long Jetty, was in walking distance from Tuggerah Lakes where we went trawling for prawns. We were also in short walking distance from Toowoon Bay. Here we skylarked and surfed and enjoyed picnics with our extended family under the shade of Norfolk Island pines. Sometimes we'd drive to the Wamberal lagoon not far from Terrigal where we and our cousins would hire canoes and paddle to our hearts' content. Sadly most of today's youth won't savour the experiences that Peter and I took for granted in those innocent and unfettered days of our youth.

Peter was the wild one. One Sunday afternoon in high summer he decided to build a raft in the backyard, using sawn-off logs secured with twine to 40-gallon drums. Our superhero's plan was to sail from Little Manly beach, up the harbour, through The Heads (the opening from Sydney harbour to the ocean) and then out to the vast beyond. Luckily for Peter, Mum caught up with him just in the nick of time – and was she furious! She was so enraged she literally took strips off him.

Peter threw himself headlong into work and golf and was soon to complete his apprenticeship with a leading firm of Sydney builders, H. W. Thompson & Company. He gained his Certificate as a Clerk of Works and laboured tirelessly on a huge building site at Circular Quay for the giant Imperial Chemical Industries (ICI). No longer was he called Peter Boy but was nicknamed Panga, and after a car accident was upgraded to Pranga. Peter was no fool when it came to the mechanics of cars as he was capable of removing the engine from his wrecked Austin A40 into its replacement.

1 The Reverend John Penman was a Primitive Methodist* and was head of the Australasian Methodist Church, now the Uniting Church in Australia. There is a distant family relationship with the former Anglican Primate of Australia and Archbishop of Melbourne, the Reverend David Penman (1936–1989).
2 The Corso, the street linking the harbour with the ocean (in Mediterranean countries, a social promenade).
3 Now the Anglican Church of Australia.

CHAPTER 2

THE TURNING POINT

Not only was Peter working hard physically on the building site during the day, he was also going to technical school at night, and having to travel from home to work and then to night school and then home again involved a lot of public transport. He'd also become passionate about learning, practising and playing golf so, lumped together, this turned out to be his eventual downfall; he was overdoing it – he was doing too much – the stress culminating in his first nervous breakdown.

It was on a late summer's afternoon in 1964 when it became apparent that Peter was losing the plot. At the time I was in the front garden of our home in Balgowlah Heights, an affluent suburb on Sydney's northern beaches. I happened to look up to see Peter walking down the road towards me appearing bewildered, but I put this down to the hot and sultry weather and the high humidity at this time of year. With his pack on his back he'd returned home by ferry and bus from the building site at Circular

Quay where he'd now been promoted to foreman. For a twenty-three-year-old he'd had lots of responsibility thrust upon him. Looking at me strangely, he glanced back over his shoulder, paused, and confided, 'There's someone following me!'

I looked towards where he was gazing and there was no-one to be seen. 'I can't see anyone, mate – you must be overtired – more likely you're exhausted. Come inside and I'll get you a glass of cold water. You've had a tough week and this humidity doesn't help.'

This is all I could think to say as I was mystified by Peter's confusion. *What am I to do now?*

Peter meandered inside and gulped down the cold water I'd taken from the refrigerator, then he stumbled towards his upstairs bedroom. Later I noticed him lying flat out on his bed in a deep sleep, snoring and totally exhausted.

It wasn't long before Mum returned from the golf club and as usual was exhausted after playing eighteen holes on this extremely taxing day. She soon began preparing our evening meal as Dad usually arrived home at about 6.30 from his office in the city. He too would be tired after his recent promotion to manager of the new branch of the Bank[1] at the recently completed high-rise AMP Building opposite Circular Quay. Should I tell Mum and Dad about my encounter with Peter?

Peter remained in his bedroom sleeping peacefully so I figured that now was the right time to tell them what had happened. I hesitated, then blurted out, 'Something's wrong with Peter!'

After I'd told them what had happened Mum said nothing, looked bewildered, then looked at Dad. Dad paused, looked at me, and in a sudden rage slapped me hard across the face – yelling at me – denying that anything was wrong: 'There's nothing wrong with *my* son!'

As he immediately strode defiantly from the kitchen I was in disbelief at what had just happened. Until that day my father had never laid a hand on me and now, close to tears, I mumbled to Mum, 'I'll never forgive my father! He doesn't care – it's all about him!'

Scurrying from the kitchen I dissolved into my room and fell disconsolately onto my bed, soaking my pillow in tears, but early the next morning, when I could hear Mum clattering about in the kitchen, I went up to her in remorse for what had happened the evening before. Giving me a big hug she gently said, as lovingly as she could muster, 'Paul, dear, you must forgive your father for his outburst. He was shocked at what you said.'

Without replying I just stood there sulking, knowing that I had to forgive my father. But not yet!

After this incident my relationship with Dad became icy. He and Mum must have had a deep and meaningful discussion about what I'd said because they arranged for an urgent appointment for Peter to be seen by Mum's psychiatrist. I recall the consultant psychiatrist as a Macquarie Street specialist, even recalling his name, Dr William Arnott, who at that time was a leading and highly respected professional in the field of psychiatric medicine.

---

1 The Bank of New South Wales, opened in 1817, was the first bank in Australia. Prior to this promotion, Dad had opened a new branch of the bank in Milson's Point on the other side of Sydney harbour.

CHAPTER 3

THE HEART-CRY OF
A MOTHER

Soon afterwards, Mum wrote the following letter to her niece in Adelaide.

14th March 1965

Dear Pat

We were pleased to receive your letter and to know you were all well. I had a month in hospital this year. Went in on New Year's Day as I was very ill, had spent most of 1964 upset over Peter. However my collapse was a blessing in disguise, for my doctor insisted on seeing Peter when he knew that was my worry. Peter has been in care ever since and is nearly well again. The doctor said he had been having a very serious breakdown for over a year. I knew there was something very astray with him but did not think it was his nerves, his Father and myself asked him to go to the doctor many times – but he would laugh and say 'I'm as fit as a fiddle.' He looked it too and could eat very well, but he had just lost his confidence, he would not go out – or to sport – and did very little work. However that is all over. The doctor said he must not do any work that would cause him to worry for a long while, so he has had work with the public works department for six weeks. He is assisting a surveyor, and this entails working in the country. He has been to Tumut for two weeks and to Adelong and for the last three weeks has been at Wollongong – of course he did surveying in his technical course, so that helps. He does not get the wages he did in the trade as he is a foreman – still he gets first class hotel expenses and 20 pounds a week – I say he is having a holiday – on pay – and best of all he is getting better.

We had some fun yesterday, a friend of mine and I invited Peter and Paul as our visitors to Balgowlah Golf Club. I played with Paul who has just taken up golf and was airing his fifty pounds' worth of golf equipment. Paul had been at a party the night before and arrived home at 4 a.m. He was not much good, but Peter played like a champion – he had four birdies and nine pars, if you know what that means. The party Paul had been to, he organised. It was 'back to the twenties' at his local tennis club – Bareena Park. The girls did a floor show and they danced the Charleston. Paul got himself up in Dad's bowling creams – red waistcoat, tie and armbands, black bowler hat and cigar – he looked very good.

I am very well again, played golf this week, Tuesday, Wednesday and Thursday – but my word I worked for a week to prepare for it.

Well, Pat – I started this letter some days ago – but it is all news. Have been out to see Myrtle – she is better. Bill has a little new 650 Morris station wagon. Their little home at Blacktown is very comfortable. I asked Bill how old you would be and he said twenty-two. I laughed and told him he was losing his memory, as you stayed with me for a week once at Maroubra and you were about three. Peter was born the next January, so I think you must be twenty-seven or eight as Peter was twenty-four last January.

Well, old love, I must away. All the best to Max, Bill and family from us all.

Love,
Auntie Thelma

Is it possible to know what's going on in another person's mind? This is the question I ponder as I flick through Peter's British/Australian passport dated 18 October 1962. At twenty-one he's

Paul, aspiring advertising executive

13

planning to travel overseas, then the dream of most young people, but he was never to leave the Australian shores. Only he knew what dark clouds were looming overhead – that black dog of depression was starting to bark. Perhaps he planned to see the world before settling down to marry and have children, or maybe he was considering running away from the demons that were taunting him? No-one will ever know.

Even though Peter and I were good friends, we had little to say to each other at the dinner table as our lives were vastly different. Peter was the tradesman, surfer and golfer and Paul was the aspiring advertising executive, tennis enthusiast and lover of life. I had no clue about what he was thinking.

CHAPTER 4

PSYCHOLOGICAL PROBLEMS IN THE FAMILY LINE

In the frenetic and volatile world of advertising[1] in the 1960s, life as an up-and-coming advertising executive took me on a quick trajectory. If not spending most of my weekends playing tennis or partying I'd be on the lookout for someone special to love, so when I finally found the love of my life, Peter was just a blot on the horizon. I was in another world and had no idea what he was up to.

I'm now twenty-four and Peter's twenty-six and I've fallen in love with a beautiful woman and today we're to be married. It's to be a grand, social, choral wedding at St Andrew's in trendy Brighton. Mum and Dad have flown down from Sydney and Mum looks really elegant, serene, refined and composed – this sixty-two-year-old woman so beautifully groomed and sporting a fox fur (borrowed from one of her golfing buddies). She's also wearing a courageous disguise as she'd only been discharged from hospital the day before, having survived yet another nervous breakdown and yet again another course of electroconvulsive therapy. Just imagine the superhuman effort she'd made to attend her son's wedding!

The day after the wedding and the love feast that followed, my new bride and I returned to her family home in East Brighton before leaving for our honeymoon in Adelaide. Here we found Mum at the kitchen table sharing stories from her childhood with my new in-laws. She was fragile and quite disturbed as she retold the tragic details, snippets of which I'd heard over the years.[2]

Mum recounted that she was a twin but it wasn't until thirty-six hours after her birth that a brother was discovered and delivered stillborn. For corrective surgery on Mum's cleft lip,[3] long journeys in a Model A Ford on dusty, potholed roads had to be manoeuvred from Caragabal in central western New South Wales to Sydney and back again. When Mum was five her mother had a total mental collapse, was diagnosed insane and spent the rest of her life in 'lunatic' asylums in Sydney, Goulburn and the Central Coast. When Mum was eighteen her mother underwent surgery for 'women's problems', the result of her confinement back in Caragabal all those years ago. She died soon afterwards. Mum would describe her mother as 'that poor unfortunate' and indeed she was. Mum's nineteen-year-old brother Bill reacted to his mother's death by burning their substantial homestead to the ground. Because of the shock of her mother's unexpected death and now being homeless, a prominent streak of grey hair appeared through Mum's long brown wavy hair overnight.

This all happened soon after Mum had returned home after spending a year at 'finishing school' down in Sydney at the Presbyterian Ladies' College in Burwood.

1 *Mad Men* is a television series that depicts the typical world of 1960s advertising in Madison Avenue, NYC. Little did I know back in the 1960s that in 1970, after a stint as Media Director of an advertising agency in Johannesburg, I was to be guest speaker at an International Media Managers' Forum in Madison Avenue at a prominent advertising agency, Doyle, Dane, Bernbach.

2 I've included this information to provide a background to the causes of the so-called 'mental illness' in our family.

3 Cleft lip – one or more splits in the upper lip that occur as a birth defect. Peter was also born with a cleft lip. I was born with a cleft lip and palate, also known as an orofacial cleft.

CHAPTER 5

WHAT'S PETER UP TO?

Let's see if I can paint a broad canvas of what Peter was doing when he came to Melbourne for his little brother's wedding.

When he returned from working in the bush Peter came to live with Dad and Mum in the family home in Balgowlah Heights. Peter had lapsed into severe depression and was unable to find work and sat around the house smoking.[1] Peter didn't use illicit drugs but only those professionally prescribed, and his consumption of alcohol was minimal. He was certainly no slouch and couldn't abide dole bludgers, so when he was well enough he wasn't a layabout and always looked for any type of work available.

Peter did a stint that lasted nine months, working as a labourer at Nabalco[2] in Gove in the Northern Territory, and later worked as a rouseabout on a dangerous maintenance job, hanging out of windows on tall buildings in Surfers Paradise. By now he could no longer hold down a permanent job, so after a near-fatal accident on one of those tall towers he had to finally hang up his tools of trade. Thus commenced his journey further into madness.

By 1974 Peter had left home and was living in a boarding house in Annie Street, Brisbane. In 1975 it's a room at an unknown address in Ipswich. In 1976 he buys a block of land in Goombungee in southern Queensland and builds himself a shack on the land, and by 1979 he's neglected to pay his land rates and the block is sold from under him.[3] He buys a 1950s Masonite caravan and is seen parked at the showground in Goombungee – and he's told to f— off! Between 1980 and 1986 Peter gravitates between caravan parks in Oakey, Esk and Crow's Nest, and in 1987 he settles his caravan on a permanent site in a caravan park in Ruthven Street, Toowoomba, a town in the heart of the prosperous Darling Downs.

1 These were the days before the illegal drug marijuana became popular. Peter smoked legal, roll-your-own cigarettes.
2 Nabalco (North Australian Bauxite and Alumina Company) – a mining and exploration company renamed in 2002.
3 I warned Peter this could happen and it did. The land sold for a pittance and someone with inside information in the County of Aubigny must have thought they'd won the lottery!

CHAPTER 6

WHAT'S DAD UP TO?

It's time to backtrack to our father, now living alone in our family home in Balgowlah Heights. Mum's in a nursing home in Wahroonga and Dad's retired. Deciding to take himself on a cruise to England, Dad immediately finds a soul mate, has a brief affair and not long afterwards clandestinely divorces his wife (our mother) and secretly marries this new woman.

Meanwhile, in the nursing home Mum has no idea she's been divorced and is now left destitute as our father has connived to have her struck out of his will.[1] Can you imagine the superannuation she was entitled to after Dad's forty-three years working in the Bank? What sort of human being would do this to his wife of over thirty-five years?

How our mother came to be in a nursing home in Wahroonga isn't hard to establish as Dad's new wife lived in Newcastle, and Wahroonga was on the highway between Newcastle and Sydney. Wahroonga is one of Sydney's most exclusive addresses and as one

WHAT'S DAD UP TO?

deceived family member was overheard saying, 'Johnnie[2] is so considerate. Wahroonga is such a lovely place for Thelma to be living.'

When Dad phoned me in Melbourne to tell me he'd moved Mum from a convalescent home[3] in Manly, I smelt a dirty big rat! Mum had recently been involved in a near-fatal car crash on her way home from the golf club and spent a long time in Manly District Hospital. When she was transferred to this convalescent home in Wood's Street I knew something was on the nose, so I took a day off work to fly to Sydney to find out what was going on.

Arriving unannounced at the nursing home, I found our mother, this formerly elegant woman, now a hardly recognisable skeleton of a person slouched on a single bed in an upstairs ward amongst similarly disembodied souls, hidden from the gaze of regular visitors. Yes. It was our precious mum.

Mosquito bites pocked her fragile face, and her complexion was pale and her body a shadow of her former tall, statuesque and elegant self. Mum's eyes opened at the sound of my familiar voice – you could tell she recognised her beloved second son. I handed her a single pink magnolia I'd especially chosen. She reached out for it, examined it closely, took it to her mouth and proceeded to eat it. I was appalled! (As I write this I start to sob – the memory is so painful... now tears start to fall.)

As I removed the magnolia from Mum's lips she looked at me blankly and with a sigh gasped, '*Who is going to look after Peter when I die?*'

At that very moment I knew I was to become my brother's keeper.

Understandably I was ropeable. How could anyone show such neglect to another human being?

Deciding then and there to get the perpetrator of this cruel act, in a rage I stormed downstairs in the hope of finding the culprit. I pushed the buzzer hard at the nurses' station, with no response. I pushed the buzzer again and again even harder and still there was no response. Finally a nurse appeared – frazzled and frightened – and did I let her have it!

'I'm Mrs Penman's son and I've come from Melbourne especially to see my mother. What the hell is going on here? I demand to see her doctor immediately. Where's the bastard?'

The cowering nurse fumbled around in her teledex, scribbled an address on a piece of paper and scurried off. The doctor's address was nearby, so without hesitation I crossed the room, ran down the stairs and in giant steps hastened to the address I'd been given. Surprise, surprise! There was no-one home. Now that I reflect on this scene I thank God for His protection at this time as who knows what I could have done in my groundswell of emotions? Murder seemed the best option!

---

1 To this day my family can't work out how this could possibly be.
2 Dad's family called him Johnnie and close friends called him Jack.
3 In 1942 this was called Wyuna, a private maternity hospital where I was born. Now it was a private convalescent home. It was recently restored to its original grandeur as a stately mansion built for a former mayor of Manly.

CHAPTER 7

MAYHEM IN MELBOURNE

In Melbourne our second gorgeous baby had arrived, but I was feeling somewhat ill at ease as my life was becoming more unsettled. My wife was struggling to cope with postnatal depression and I wasn't coping in my demanding position as Media Director of an advertising agency. With a gypsy in Peter's soul he'd gone walkabout and no-one knew where he was or even seemed to care. Dad was madly in love and seemed to be oblivious to the unfolding melodrama.

I gave Dad an earful on the phone about our mother's dire situation in the nursing home. By now he'd sold our family home in Balgowlah Heights and had bought a substantial two-storey house in dress circle Merewether Heights, a Newcastle suburb that overlooked the sea with expansive views of this industrial city. Dad was soon to come clean on how he came to divorce our mother. He'd met a lady on his overseas trip and when he returned home boasted (to me) that he'd found a mistress. But this mistress was very keen to be made Mrs Penman; consequently, as has already been shared, Dad had to divorce our mother to marry this new woman – but in the process he neglected to inform his wife!

It was happy hour in the lounge room of the new love-nest overlooking the glittering lights of Newcastle when Dad, after a few whiskeys, eventually replied to my vitriolic earful, 'Paul. If you don't like the nursing home where I've placed your mother, you'll have to move her yourself.'

This is just what I didn't need to hear: yet another example of my father abrogating his responsibility.

After a lot of toing and froing in the days that followed, my father came to a financial arrangement with Mum's brother's wife Myrtle[1] to look after Mum in their ramshackle Fibrolite cottage in Blacktown, a depressing suburb west of Sydney. Of course it was I who had to again obtain compassionate leave from my responsible position in Melbourne to fly to Sydney to accompany Mum in the ambulance as she was transferred from the Wahroonga nursing home to Blacktown.

1 You were introduced to Myrtle in Chapter 3.

CHAPTER 8

A TRAGEDY DIVERTED
IN SYDNEY

Somehow Mum did find out she was no longer Mrs Penman. She'd been divorced by her husband of over thirty-five years and soon she began to wallow in grief. Shortly after she settled into the house in Blacktown, she dived headlong into a profoundly deep depression where she remained. No antidepressant drugs or grief counselling could rescue her.

Early one morning, after Mum had been in Blacktown for a month, Myrtle heard a noise in the kitchen and hurried out of bed to find Mum with the cutlery drawer open and brandishing a carving knife raised above her head and pointing to her heart. In complete shock Myrtle grabbed the knife and immediately phoned my father. She was quickly admitted to the Blacktown Nursing Home where she remained for some years until her death in 1977. In spite of what her death certificate read, the cause was her broken heart: a woman betrayed by the husband she had loved and trusted for so long.

CHAPTER 9

FAMILIAL RELATIONSHIPS AT BREAKING POINT

At an advertising industry function in Melbourne. Paul next to Lady Joy Snedden with Sir Billy Snedden looking on

After Mum's death my home life, my working life and my sporting life in Melbourne became a nightmare. In late 1977 I was head-hunted from positions as a media buying influential in advertising agencies to selling advertising space in the mass media owned by the Packer family.[1] Ita Buttrose had hit the

Paul with relative Henri Verbrugghen in St. Paul, USA

headlines as editor of the salacious magazine *Cleo* and after its spectacular success was promoted to the position of editor at Australia's largest circulating women's magazine, *The Australian Women's Weekly*, and I was appointed to sell advertising space in its controversial new A4 format reduced from its traditional tabloid size. This was a really tough assignment but I succeeded in convincing the major national advertisers with headquarters in Melbourne to remain faithful to the old girl! News of my success came to the ears of Rupert Murdoch's men on mahogany row in the Surry Hills head office, so in 1978 I was again headhunted and was appointed Victorian Representative for the (Sydney) *Sunday Telegraph*, Murdoch's Australian cash cow and second largest circulating newspaper in Australia.[2] In this new role success followed success, but there was a downside – unhappiness at home. Achieving unparalleled sales figures, I decided my wife and I could run away together to get a breath of fresh air. It seemed a good idea to visit Murdoch's newspapers in New York and San

Paul handing out prizes at the Royal South Yarra
Tennis Club in Melbourne

Francisco, so here was an opportunity to give us both a short break from life in Melbourne and have a second romantic honeymoon overseas. But my wife wouldn't leave the children (now aged eight and four) in the capable hands of her mother who lived nearby.

Deciding not to come with me turned out to be a huge mistake. I just had to get away, which medicos call a normal 'fight or flight' response to sustained pressure. Just a peek at my passport photo showed I was heading for trouble as I'd grown a beard and was becoming confused and depressed, though this didn't prevent me from having a ball while I was away.

I became what's known on the circuit as a tennis groupie and was made welcome at Wimbledon by an old friend from Manly days, John Alexander, and joined his entourage as he competed at Forest Hills[3] in New York. I was welcomed at the Murdoch newspapers and travelled by Greyhound bus across America, visiting relatives in Montana on the way. After arriving home to

an extremely resentful household, I returned to my office and phoned Murdoch's general manager and resigned. My family was my first priority so I chose them over my career, a decision I've never regretted.

My relationship with my father was now on a knife-edge. At Christmas each year my little family would drive to Newcastle to spend some of our summer holidays. Peter would make the journey from wherever he was living at the time, and special rules were enforced because of his addiction to nicotine. We only saw him at mealtimes as he confined himself to the downstairs living room where he slept for much of the day. He said nothing about Dad's new wife nor did he ever mention our mother's death, even though he'd attended the funeral which I'd been delegated to totally organise.

Many years and many Christmases in Newcastle passed. Our children were oblivious to what was happening behind the scenes, so from their perspective Christmas holidays by the sea with Grandpa were filled with fun and frolic.

1 The Packer dynasty: Robert Clyde (1879–1934); (Sir) Frank (1906–1974); Kerry (1937–2005); James (1967–present).
2 Today the (Sydney) *Sunday Telegraph* is Australia's largest circulating and most widely read newspaper.
3 Until 1978 Forest Hills was the home of the US Open. I saw Ken Rosewall play one of his finer matches here. The US Open is now played at Flushing Meadow Park, also in the borough of Queens.

CHAPTER 10

THE DEATH OF OUR DAD

In 1990 an abrupt end came to fun and frolic when Grandpa suffered a massive heart attack. The news was relayed through his new wife's daughter and by then my relationship with her and her family had become fractious. I was told, 'Don't come to Newcastle – there's no hope – the heart attack was fatal.'

Naturally I was shocked when I received this news but I had a deep-seated desire to see Dad before he died, so the next morning I phoned the Royal Newcastle Hospital direct and was told he had regained consciousness and was now lucid. I was on the first possible flight to Newcastle and found him in the emergency ward, sitting up in his bed waiting for me.

'I've had a good innings[1] – I've lived to eighty,' he said, 'and everything must come to an end.' He paused and continued, 'Paul, would you give me a shave and would you feed me my breakfast?'

As a dutiful son honouring his father to the end, I shaved him his last shave and fed him his last breakfast as we both knew he would die later that day. His last words to me were, 'You've seen my Will. I have to provide for my [new] wife but I've made provision for both of you boys – and don't fight over the petty cash.'

Having no idea what he was referring to when he talked about the petty cash, I responded, 'Yes, Dad. I'm not interested in your Will or the petty cash.'

After kissing Dad on his freshly shaven cheek and saying my last goodbye, I returned to Melbourne. In the afternoon he died. Later we were to discover that even as he lay on his deathbed and uttered his last words, he'd lied: when the Will was finally read Peter and I had been almost totally excluded – there wasn't a cent for Peter and a few dud shares for me. I wasn't perturbed because for many years I'd had a sense that I would never inherit from my father. And here's why…

Some months after our mother's death I wrote Dad a long, scathing letter telling him what I thought of him, especially when he abandoned Mum and then divorced her on the quiet and remarried. I recall writing the letter in tears, concluding that I still loved him in spite of what he'd done to Mum. I was to discover later that this letter went down like a lead balloon! No doubt encouraged by his new wife, he immediately changed his Will, leaving Peter with nothing and Paul with the petty cash. How do I know? The executor of the Will was changed from Dad's brother, Neville Penman, a highly respected solicitor in Gosford. And guess who replaced him? Aha! You guessed it! Dad's new wife's son-in-law! (You don't need to be Albert Einstein to work out who was behind this great deception.)

I'd made my own way in life so I was financially secure, but for Peter's sake I decided to contest the Will. This decision came to naught, even though I obtained Legal Aid through a Sydney solicitor that meant more flying trips backwards and forwards to Sydney from Melbourne. Unsurprisingly the Newcastle cupboard was found to be literally bare. The house had been quickly sold and so had the huge share portfolio. Paintings, expensive furniture and other valuable possessions had miraculously vanished. Therefore, according to the Sydney solicitor, the Will was not worth contesting.

---

1 This is a cricket expression which Dad often used. In his halcyon days he was captain of the Western New South Wales cricket team and often boasted that his team played against 'our Don Bradman'.

CHAPTER 11

PETER'S JOURNEY CONTINUES

At last we can now follow Peter's journey after the death of our father. As I've written, Peter had said nothing about our father's new wife, nor had he much to say about our mother's death during or after her funeral. He was suffering in silence. He'd withdrawn from society and into himself, and by 1991 he'd escaped to Toowoomba where I found him at death's door. At the time I too was in a state of transition as my volatile career in advertising had ended abruptly in 1984 when I'd been working with the Fairfax media. At last, thank God, my twenty-five years in this soul-destroying, cut-throat profession were over. For the next few years I worked part-time in a number of occupations, including store-housing and tennis coaching, and by 1990 I'd enrolled full-time at Swinburne University of Technology in Hawthorn, in the arts faculty, to study for the degree of Bachelor of Arts in Media. For me this was a real game change.

Far too early one cold, wet and windy winter's morning, right in the midst of this work and cultural shift, the phone rang.

I fell out of bed to hear an almost incoherent sound – it was Peter's almost incoherent voice and he was obviously drunk. There was no need to say it; this was an urgent plea for help – something was seriously wrong up in Queensland. I suspended my university studies immediately, put my affairs in order and drove the 1,200 kilometres to Toowoomba in my old faithful station wagon with my old faithful dog Raz by my side. I wrote the following letter after I arrived:

> Writing from Toowoomba Caravan Park
> 821 Ruthven Street
> Toowoomba, Queensland

> Dear Concerned Family Members,

> For the time being I've had to pull out from mainstream life to care for Peter. I've withdrawn from all university studies and have also deferred my tennis examinations[1] which were being held at the Australian Institute of Sport in Canberra. Now my priorities are vastly different. As you know, last week I had a distress signal from Peter so I dropped everything and now I'm here indefinitely. I couldn't believe what I was seeing when I arrived here late last Friday as I was shocked to the core.

35

I found Peter in his caravan, barefoot and wearing a dirty singlet and shorts, bizarre clothing for this time of year. The poor man was unshaven, his hair uncombed and dishevelled. He greeted me as though I was an answer to prayer (which of course I was). He held out his hand to greet me and, just like our dear departed mother, was a skeleton of his former self. 'G'day, little brother... how's the trip... much traffic on the road?'

He knew I'd come to his aid – it was just a matter of when... the faithful little brother he could always depend on.

We went inside his home, the 16-foot Fibrolite caravan with no annex and threadbare just like its occupant.
Peter opened the door of his tiny refrigerator to reveal a single bottle of milk. 'Want a cuppa?'
'Yes, why not?'

(I wondered how long the opened bottle of milk had been there and how recently the jar of instant coffee sitting on the kitchen bench had been opened.) Peter was in a daze and must have been highly medicated as he put six teaspoons of white sugar into his black coffee.
'I haven't slept for a week, Paul – I'm up shit creek without a paddle. What's going to happen to me?'

He paused, began to cry and then there was silence. This was a dire situation so I tried my best not to cry too.

After we'd drunk our coffee Peter composed himself and, now enlivened by the caffeine hit, continued, 'A few weeks ago I was beaten up by two coppers; I wasn't doing anything wrong, all I was doing was having a beer in the pub down the road and keeping to myself. They just set upon me, accusing me of staring at them. They dragged me into the alley next to the pub and beat the crap out of me, then they took me to the police station and I was charged with beating them up and I've been fined $800 for assaulting them.' After a deep sigh he continued, 'And another thing happened. About two weeks ago in the middle of the day I was on my way to McDonald's and minding my own business when two teenagers crept up behind me, bashed me and stole my wallet and now I think I've begun to haemorrhage.'

Peter was in crisis: brain damage, malnutrition, zombied out of his brain with drugs prescribed by the local psychiatrist, delirious and now hallucinating. My big brother is at death's door!

I did what I always do in situations too difficult for me to handle – I prayed to the Lord and the obvious solution came immediately: '*Take Peter straight away to the Emergency Department at the local hospital.*'

So, dear family, that's where I'm up to. I'll keep you posted on what happens. Please continue to pray for both of us.

May God bless all of you.

(Signed) Paul

After a thorough examination Peter was admitted to the psychiatric unit at the Toowoomba Base Hospital where he remained for six months.

1 Level 3 Elite Accreditation.

CHAPTER 12

SOME LIGHT RELIEF FROM THIS UNFOLDING DRAMA

By this time my wife Beverley and I had separated so I moved into Peter's caravan for the entire period he was in the psychiatric unit. I spent my spare time volunteering with the local Pentecostal* church and joined the Toowoomba Tennis Club, playing A Grade in representative matches, even playing singles in a mid-winter tournament in freezing Crow's Nest.

Needing some intellectual stimulation I enrolled at the University of Southern Queensland where I continued the Arts degree I'd put on hold in Melbourne, but such were the emotionally draining circumstances I soon had to withdraw.

Instead, unadvisedly, I took on a different challenge by representing a fledgling newspaper, *The Toowoomba Advertiser*. Years beforehand I'd been appointed Advertising Manager of the long-established *Toowoomba Chronicle* but had to decline that offer due to issues with Beverley's family, so to have a similar opportunity now held great appeal.

With my entrepreneurial hat firmly on, I established a media consultancy which I named Paul Penman and Associates, the business name I'd registered many years ago in Melbourne when I was gravitating between full-time and self-employment. How the consultancy came to be established is quite a hoot as I'll now explain. You'll enjoy reading the next bit.

Toowoomba is renowned for its annual Carnival of Flowers festival, held in spring in their spectacular Queen's Park. I heard through my newly created network of contacts that a Home Show was to be held for the first time this year, so the organisers must need a publicity officer, mustn't they? I talked myself into the position and was soon their publicist.

I rented a small office, subsidised by the Toowoomba regional council, and soon began the publicity machine. Now I was truly in my element. My professional life had required me to be skilled at buying commercial advertising time on radio and advertising space in newspapers, magazines and the strategically placed public media, so I was more than qualified to make a significant contribution to the promotion of this new event. Wasn't it going to be a fun-filled field day!

But there was no media budget, which presented a huge problem, so, with my copywriting skills honed, I began to pen teaser press releases and advertorials[1] for the *Toowoomba Chronicle*, *Toowoomba Advertiser*, ABC Radio and the commercial radio stations. Cheekily I suggested to the mayor of Toowoomba, Clive Berghofer, that as a publicity stunt he could be flown by helicopter to open the event.[2] He agreed enthusiastically so I contacted the Brisbane television stations, encouraging them to cover the event, hopefully to be telecast at prime viewing time. All went according to plan in the preliminary stages but, woe is me, the heavens opened on the evening before the grand opening and rain bucketed down throughout the night. *What am I going to do now?*

Taking a huge punt, I scrambled out of bed in the caravan, drove in the dark to my office in Little Street and quickly scrawled a new radio advertorial in which I spruiked,

THESE FEW DROPS OF RAIN HAVEN'T SPOILED
OUR HOME SHOW!
IT'S ON!
THE HOME SHOW IN QUEEN'S PARK TODAY IS
DEFINITELY *ON.*
COME ONE, COME ALL. ROLL UP. ROLL UP.
WE WON'T LET A FEW DROPS OF RAIN SPOIL
OUR PARADE.

Thank God that as I was hand-delivering my scrawl at 5 a.m. to the radio stations the rain had stopped. Tarpaulins had to be dropped in the main thoroughfares on the lawns of Queen's Park and right on schedule a helicopter could be heard flying overhead. One startled young mum was caught in amazement as it landed: 'Look, it's the Mayor, Mr Berghofer! Wow. How fantastic! And who's that with him?'

After the excitement of the day was over and record crowds had descended upon Queen's Park in response to the radio hype, I called in to see my incredulous brother at Doonside, the halfway house Peter had moved in to after his long stint in hospital. Peter was wide-eyed and open-mouthed when he exclaimed, 'Paul – I've just seen you on television!'

Yes, there's no show without Punch! I'd managed to get myself into the evening news on Brisbane television.

Just for fun I've reproduced here an edited version of the letter I wrote to Mr Berghofer at the close of the day:

PAUL PENMAN & ASSOCIATES
Media Consultants
Toowoomba Enterprise Centre, 4 Little Street,
Toowoomba

The Mayor of the City of Toowoomba
Alderman Clive Berghofer
Council Chambers
153 Herries Street
Toowoomba

Dear Clive

This is a simple personal note to thank you for the excellent example you set your people yesterday in every aspect of your participation at the Home Show. As you know, we had excellent coverage on the television news last evening and the Home Show is now 'the talk of the town'.

This is my first business venture in a new city and, whilst I'm always a controversial person, you may be assured that I will always seek to uphold Christian values.

You have here a most magnificent city and I'm certainly pleased to be able to say that now I'm a small part of it.

Yours most sincerely

(Signed) Paul Penman

The downside of this true story is that I was never paid for all the publicity I'd created as I'd come to a gentlemen's agreement[3] with the Home Show organiser to be paid a fee of $1,000 for my contribution to the staging of this event.

At the time I was living hand to mouth, paying rent in Peter's caravan as well as the downtown office, so I wasn't even managing to exist on unemployment benefits. I reluctantly decided to take the organiser to court but was told that a gentlemen's agreement doesn't hold water in a court of law, so I had to write this off as just another of life's experiences.

Peter's caravan and his wreck of a car were eventually sold by the State Trustees whom I'd previously arranged to have his financial and private affairs administered. Shortly afterwards I arranged for his name to be placed on the waiting list for public housing.

1 An advertising campaign dressed up as press releases.
2 Clive was a prominent real-estate agent so he knew the value of advertising and arrived with his very attractive personal assistant.
3 An informal and legally non-binding agreement between two or more parties and usually sealed with a handshake.

CHAPTER 13

HOMELESS AND PENNILESS

Here follows the most dramatic period of my life. Hang on to your hats!

After the events enumerated so far, the thought of returning permanently to Melbourne didn't appear to be an option.

I too, like Peter, began wandering the King's Highway,[1] hoping to run away from an almost unbearable recent past. But the problem was... I took myself with me! For six months I lived at Currendina Lodge, a backpackers' hostel in Lismore in northern New South Wales where I managed to get work on a part-time basis. Then, on a trip to Queensland to visit Peter, I met a Christian woman in Brisbane and fell instantly in love. Love at last? As this seemed to be the real deal, it wasn't long before I rushed in and proposed marriage and my new fancy came to live with me in Lismore. Even though my feelings for her were ridgy-didge[2] I was made fully aware that our intimacy was well outside the perfect will of God. Call me a prude but my Christian upbringing often tweaked my conscience. To marry meant to divorce my wife of over twenty years, but that wasn't an option after what Dad had done to Mum. Through a set of amazing circumstances[3] I soon realised I'd jumped into bed too early and so we parted company – and certainly not amicably. I returned briefly to Melbourne, then moved to Adelaide where I remained for six months and where I was pampered by my cousin Patricia, who coincidentally was experiencing extreme unhappiness in her own life.

When I did eventually return to Melbourne to attend my daughter's twenty-first birthday, I became a couch surfer. For the first month I lived in a room in Mount Waverley, the following month in a room in a Christian brother's house in Scoresby. After that I lived with Kevin and Marilyn, a compassionate and understanding Christian married couple; my room in their tiny office-cum-sewing room was to become my refuge from the world for three more months.

During this time my wife and I arranged to meet in the hope of a permanent reconciliation. I recall two meetings, one in Adelaide and one in Sydney where we shared a meal in a coffee shop at Circular Quay overlooking the familiar Manly ferry wharf and Sydney harbour. We talked, we reminisced, we cried, but significantly we forgave each other. Oh how sadly though, when I was living in Adelaide, she had divorce papers served on me. That day my heart was torn in two as I signed the papers reluctantly. Our large family home in Mount Waverley was then sold, enabling me to purchase a permanent dwelling. I needed somewhere to hang my hat and to finally end this soul-destroying, merry-go-round saga.

Now my former wife bought a modest house in a less affluent part of Mount Waverley and our younger daughter moved in with her. I paid a deposit on what some called a gentleman's residence, a three-bedroom home unit in Atherton Road in the adjacent suburb, Oakleigh. I took on a huge mortgage, but fortuitously the timing was perfect for our older daughter to rent it from me, as she had just become engaged and we both agreed it would be a good idea for her to live independently for a while before marriage.

Thus I was homeless again but, trusting God all the way, I soon found myself living rent-free in a large, two-storey house in Sandells Road in Tecoma, a pretty place amongst undulating hills on the highway to the Dandenong ranges. This was owned by my friend Glenn, one of the leaders at the Oakleigh Christian Centre where I was worshipping at the time.

In Toowoomba, Peter had great difficulty settling in at Doonside as he felt very uncomfortable there, so, fully aware of my responsibility to our mother to oversee his care, I made a huge effort to keep in touch with him on a regular basis.

One visit to Toowoomba stands out. Peter had regular appointments with a psychiatrist and on one occasion I decided to accompany him. We were shown into a small office to await her arrival, a serious woman in her late thirties, a photo of whom, with her two children, sat prominently on the desk in front of us. I introduced myself, then she turned to Peter.

'How are you, Peter?'

Peter replied, 'I've been crying a lot lately.'

To which she responded, 'What sort of tears were they, Peter?'

Hesitatingly Peter replied, 'I've been crying because I've never married and I haven't had children.'

By now Peter was well enough to travel unaccompanied, so in the following year I organised a week's holiday together in a rented apartment in Surfers Paradise, one of his former stamping grounds. The following year I arranged to meet him in Sydney where we stayed in a youth hostel in Glebe. In the third year, because I wanted to stay in touch with what was happening at Doonside, I got my reliable Toyota into gear, and with my trustworthy dog Raz again at my side I drove the long winding road to Toowoomba to check up on him.

1 The title of a popular song made famous by Adelaide-born bass-baritone and songwriter Peter Dawson.
2 Colloquial. Australian slang for genuine, true. This word originated in southern Queensland in the 1950s.
3 Dear reader, if we ever happen to meet, ask me about the extraordinary circumstances that were to prevent me from divorcing my wife.

CHAPTER 14

THAT WOMAN'S CRAZY!

Due to my unfortunate circumstances at this stage of my life, I found myself asset rich but cash poor. Years ago when money wasn't an issue, I'd joined the Youth Hostels Association (YHA) as a Life Member, which turned out to be a wise decision as driving backwards and forwards to see Peter was costing me an arm and a leg – accommodation, petrol, and fast and slow food were very expensive. At that time there was no youth hostel in Toowoomba and motels such as the Coachman, the Hyde Park Plaza, the Riverview or even Vasey Hall were all out of the question. The option of renting a cabin at the caravan park in Ruthven Street where Peter had lived was beyond the pale – even the thought gave me the horrors. So reluctantly, I enquired about staying Doonside, and after much mucking around the manager begrudgingly permitted me to stay. In 1992 I'd transferred from Swinburne University of Technology to Tabor Bible College in Ringwood where I'd begun a Bachelor of Arts degree in Intercultural Studies with a focus on Christian mission. Unknowingly, the studies at Tabor prepared me for the huge spiritual battle that was just about to be fought in Toowoomba.

Have you ever been into a place and sensed there was something wrong but you couldn't put your finger on it – you had this strange feeling about the place? That's precisely how I felt entering Doonside. My studies at Bible College, which had prepared me for my mission to Africa, had made me conscious of the reality of the demonic realm,* and a manifestation of witchcraft* known in much of Africa as a ruling spirit* is what I'm just about to face here in Toowoomba. If a Christian wants to encounter evil spirits head-on, all that's required is to preach the Word of God.* It wasn't my intention to stir up the forces of evil,* but that's just what I did when I decided to bunk in there.

I'd reached Goondiwindi[1] where I'd stayed overnight on my long drive from Melbourne, so I phoned Doonside, informing them of my anticipated time of arrival. The phone was answered in a sweet voice by a woman who called herself Helen, announcing herself as the cook.

'Peter doesn't live here any more. He's moved.' With that she promptly hung up.

Knowing she was lying I took no notice and arrived late in the afternoon, to be settled in by the manager. Proceeding to the lounge room I was welcomed by a friendly group of mainly older ladies so I enquired, 'Would any of you ladies like me to read a few passages from the Bible?'

There were a few nods and surprised faces, so I opened the Word of God at Psalm 23 which I knew would be familiar. This went down well with those who were not asleep in their chairs. At five o'clock it was time for tea, so one of the dear ladies showed me to the dining room where I sat next to an unsavoury old codger who, reeking of wine (he was a well-known local wino who'd just walked in off the street), introduced himself as Billy the Kid. Feeling compassion for this fellow I went to the counter, where a pretty woman, probably in her late forties, was dishing out the meals. By the sound of her voice I knew this must be Helen, so as she was dishing out my meal I said, 'Hello, I'm Peter Penman's brother. You said he'd left but he's still here! I'll be staying here for a few days.' Then I quickly added, 'That poor fellow sitting next to me's in a bad way; I'm going to serve him my meal first.'

Looking daggers at me and staring at Billy, she angrily bellowed for all to hear, 'That drunk, that reprobate, have nothing to do with him, give me back that meal!'

I took absolutely no notice, took the meal out of her hands and walked back to our table. You could have cut the atmosphere with a knife, and silence now reigned supreme.

Helen was furious and stormed out of the kitchen with a carving knife in her outstretched hand. 'I'm the f—in' boss around here and I'm gonna shove this knife through your guts!'

49

She then dashed at me, threatening me three times to do just that. I jumped to my feet and with great authority commanded, 'In the name of Jesus Christ put down that knife at once.'

She put down the knife instantly and fled to the kitchen in full view of the nonplussed audience.

A note to those still following this melodrama. Here's your chance to start a rumour that this 'Paul Penman' bloke is a ratbag! The whole notion of the demonic realm, witchcraft and ruling spirits is absurd and it's all a load of rubbish – or is it? Now spend some time reading what the experts say:

> When evil spirits act in a rage, they act as a combination of the maddest and most wicked persons in existence, but all their evil is done with fullest intelligence and purpose. They know what they do, they know it is evil, terribly evil, and they will do it. They do it with rage, and with the full swing of malice, enmity and hatred. They act with fury and bestiality, like an enraged bull, as if they had no intelligence, and yet with full intelligence they carry on their work, showing the wickedness of their wickedness. They act from an absolutely depraved nature, with diabolical fury, and with an undeviating perseverance. They act with determination, persistence, and with skilful methods, forcing themselves upon mankind, upon the Church, and still more upon the spiritual man.
>
> Jessie Penn-Lewis with Evan Roberts, *War on the Saints*, unabridged edition, 1912

I left the dining room with the residents still in disbelief at what they'd just witnessed, and drove straight to the Toowoomba police station where I was advised to complete a Statement of

Witness. This I did and then returned to Doonside in order to pacify some of the residents still dazed by the incident. Peter took it all in his stride. Maybe he'd been exposed to this type of behaviour before.

My Statement of Witness to the Queensland Police Service was a waste of my valuable time as no charges were laid. There would be no follow-up, which was no surprise to me as the 1980s saw the dying embers of Joh Bjelke-Petersen's nineteen-year reign as Premier of Queensland and the well overdue Fitzgerald inquiry into police corruption. As a result of the inquiry, former Queensland Police Commissioner Terry Lewis was convicted and jailed for ten years.

But I wasn't a happy chappy! If that madwoman had a go at me – this strong, fit and feisty male – with a carving knife, what havoc could she provoke amongst those less strong and courageous! So I decided to act as the residents' emissary and on my next trip to Queensland made an appointment to see the local Member of Parliament Mike Horan, who at the time was representing the seat of Toowoomba South in the Legislative Assembly. Interestingly, Mike had replaced Clive Berghofer.

Mike was an inspiration as he listened attentively to everything I had to say, taking lots of notes and assuring me he'd look into the matter, so I left Toowoomba knowing I'd met a battler's friend.

A couple of weeks later I received a letter from Mr Horan which read in part: 'Further to our recent meeting, we have followed up your concern about the alleged attack at Doonside by the woman known as Helen. We wish to inform you that Helen has since died.'

You might think I was shocked to receive the news of Helen's sudden death but I wasn't at all surprised. Turning to the Scriptures, we read in Psalm 105:15,

Do not touch my anointed ones; do my prophets no harm.

And we read in Romans 12:19,

Do not take revenge, my friends, but leave room for God's wrath, for it is written:[2] 'It is mine to avenge; I will repay, says the Lord.'

And further, in Malachi 3:5,

'So I will come near to you for judgment. I will be quick to testify against sorcerers, adulterers[3] and perjurers, against those who defraud labourers of their wages, who oppress the widows and the fatherless, and deprive aliens of justice, but do not fear me,' says the LORD Almighty.

---

1 The name Goondiwindi derives from an Aboriginal word meaning 'the resting place of the birds'.
2 Deuteronomy 32:35.
3 It was confirmed later that Helen had been having an affair with the married manager at Doonside.

CHAPTER 15

A BREATH OF FRESH AIR

Peter with Paul's dog 'Raz'

Valued reader, thanks for keeping up with me so far. It's been a long and winding road but there's light at the end of the tunnel.

After more than a year on the waiting list Peter was offered emergency public housing through the Queensland Department of Housing and Public Works. He knocked back the first offer, which was of great concern to me, but accepted the second in a bedsitter located in one of the best locations in Toowoomba.

Visitors from all over Australia marvel at the panoramic views from the peak of Table Top Mountain, which overlooks the city from the nature reserve just up the road from Groom Lodge in Ipswich Street where Peter was now to live. At last Peter was able to have the security of a permanent roof over his head, and for a while his physical and mental health improved. He bought a bicycle and started to take an interest in his pocket-handkerchief garden, even winning the council's garden competition. I arranged for him to join the Senior Citizens' Club[1] where he was very popular and was twice runner-up in their indoor bowls competition. Peter remained at Groom Lodge for three years until 1997 when he was to have his next nervous breakdown.

---

1 I had an ally in their honorary secretary who was such a caring person. We corresponded regularly so I could keep tabs on Peter.

CHAPTER 16

ANOTHER CRISIS IN
TOOWOOMBA

No-one likes to receive a phone call at an ungodly hour and I've had a few. This call came at 4 a.m. As Peter's voice was hardly recognisable I knew this was yet another cry for help and little brother was being called to the rescue. His words were almost indistinguishable so I knew to say, 'Hold on, mate. I'll be there as soon as I can. Don't do anything silly.'

The problem was I was skint. In 1995 I'd returned from a short mission to Africa and was only just recovering financially. I told my elder daughter and her husband about my dilemma who came to the rescue immediately and gave me enough money to travel to Toowoomba by overnight coach, a gruelling journey in anyone's language. They separately arranged with a Toowoomba supermarket to have an emergency supply of food delivered to Peter at Groom Lodge.

When I eventually arrived in Toowoomba I found Peter almost incoherent. The food hadn't been touched and the place was in a

Paul with 'Raz'.

mess. With the last of the funds generously given to me I phoned for a taxi and soon Peter and I were in the emergency department of the Toowoomba Base Hospital where Peter was admitted. The next day I made an appointment to see their social worker who agreed it was time for Peter to be resettled in Melbourne to be closer to those who cared about him.

Now came the task of closing down his bedsit at Groom Lodge and disposing of Peter's possessions. I gave his refrigerator to his most thankful next-door neighbour, and the rest of his chattels I donated to a local Christian charity. These actions were agreed to by the State Trustees handling Peter's finances.

CHAPTER 17

WHERE'S PETER GOING TO LIVE?

What *are we going to do with Peter now?* He can no longer live alone, he has no money and can only just exist on his disability pension. So what do you do in this situation? You pray.

At the time of this latest crisis I was living in Warburton, a town about 75 kilometres north-east of Melbourne. I was doing postgraduate study at Swinburne University in Lilydale, so to find suitable accommodation there was a logical option. I prayed for God's guidance and ran it past my son-in-law who confirmed Lilydale as the place. Soon negotiations were finalised and Lilydale Lodge, an assisted accommodation house in Clarke Street, became Peter's Victorian home.

The managers of Lilydale Lodge were a kindly married couple and did their utmost to look after Peter. I was able to call in to see him at least twice a week as my university schedule allowed, but I was again ill at ease. I had to make frequent trips with Peter to Maroondah Hospital in nearby Ringwood due to various physical emergencies, as by then he was having to take a bundle of prescribed medications which were doing him no good, in fact they were sending him off his rocker.

CHAPTER 18

THE NURSING HOME FIASCO

After too many trips backwards and forwards to the outpatients department at Maroondah Hospital, I was coming to my wits' end. It's time to consider a place where Peter can get more individual care.

Silvan Country Cottage sounded quaint. The lovely Dandenongs – what bliss this could be for Peter! Set in picturesque surroundings, this special accommodation facility seemed to be a logical stepping stone, but unfortunately Peter was becoming increasingly psychotic and when I was told that he'd been taking all his clothes off and walking around naked I was flummoxed. *What am I to do now?*

Canterbury Road Lodge in Ringwood turned out to be the next disaster. Having to live at such close quarters with other demented residents and to have to share a room with another significantly deranged person… I knew it was time to bite the bullet and to move Peter yet again.

Healesville & District Private Nursing Home in Don Road became yet another disastrous move. Only 30 kilometres from Warburton and set in rugged bushland, this seemed a sensible option at the time. My many fears for Peter's mental and physical well-being proved to be well founded when, soon after Peter was admitted, the distressed proprietor informed me that Peter kept walking out of the property in the middle of the day onto the main road. This facility was positioned on a sharp bend in the winding narrow road and Peter would stand in a blind spot playing Russian roulette[1] with the oncoming traffic. How he wasn't knocked over or killed is impossible to fathom.

In desperation I again cried out to the Lord. 'Oh God... won't You please take Peter home to be with You? His life has become unbearable. Why have You allowed him to go through this torment for all these years? What am I to do?'

1 An action that is potentially very dangerous.

CHAPTER 19

MY LAST RESORT

Unless you've actually experienced looking after someone like Peter you've probably no idea what I'm going through. It's 2003 and I've moved into a house in Warburton for a tree change,[1] and Karenina Lodge is the name I elect to give to my spacious western red cedar split-level home. I've called my place after Russian author Leo Tolstoy's classic work of faith literature[2] *Anna Karenina*. Ostensibly I make the move from Melbourne to escape the life in the suburbs, but to be truthful I'm running away from the vicissitudes of life. I end up being busier than ever, symptomatic of 'doing' rather than 'being', to avoid the trials and tribulations I was having while overseeing Peter's ongoing care.

By now, those who are still journeying with me will confirm my credo *I'd rather wear out than rust*. I'm now over sixty and on the cusp of retirement so you'd expect a normal person to slow down and smell the roses. Not me! I continued my postgraduate studies at Swinburne University where I was briefly a member of staff, supervising a student for his Honours degree. I began teaching tennis part-time and soon was appointed coach at the Wandin Tennis Club, the Yarra Junction Tennis Club, and the Warburton Tennis Club where I was to be elected president in their centenary year. I was also appointed Tennis Professional at the Seventh-day Adventists' Warburton Health Resort, and on Saturday mornings I coached privately at the popular indoor tennis centre in Mount Evelyn.

If that wasn't enough I was elected to the Vestry of the Warburton Anglican church, St Mary's, and in due course began Blokes' Brunch, an outreach to the many lost souls in the Upper Yarra, particularly in the isolated caravan parks in Yarra Junction and Warburton. My watering hole was a local bar called The Beach where I imbibed much amber fluid and got to know the locals well.

Thrown into this mix was a disquiet within me as Peter's life was now in turmoil. *I have to do something – but what?*

'Oh Lord, these drug cocktails, this lack of exercise, this institutional food and his chronic depression, his chronic schizophrenia and his recently diagnosed frontal lobe dementia add up to a time bomb with the fuse lit and ready to explode. I don't want Peter to die in one of these places. If it's his time to come home to You, I want him to die here, at home, with me.'

(Note, I didn't ask the Lord what I should do; I told Him what *I* was going to do! Big mistake.)

1 A phrase used to describe a move from living in the city to a more rural/country and hopefully serene lifestyle.
2 This book provides a wonderful illustration of man's faith and trust in God.

CHAPTER 20

MY BIGGEST MISTAKE

You'll recall that before I took the deviation from Peter's journey to tell you about Warburton, Peter was playing Russian roulette in Healesville. There were to be no problems moving him on; in fact they no longer knew how to handle him so I was doing them a favour by taking him to live with me.

Before I'd made the decision for Peter to live with me (in the hope of restoring my own sanity), I took myself on a three months' holiday and in the year 2000 travelled to every mainland capital in Australia with my old school buddy John. (Can't you see the lengths I've gone to avoid the reality of Peter's plight!) At the time, Qantas had a great deal operating, so we flew from Melbourne to Sydney, Brisbane, Cairns, Darwin, Alice Springs, Perth, Adelaide and then home to Melbourne.

Shortly afterwards I packed my bags and headed for scintillating Sydney where I visited my elder daughter and her husband,

and my first grandchild, who were now living and working there. I found a full-time position working with a newspaper in North Ryde called *The Weekly Times* and after some disagreements early in my employment I found myself wrongfully dismissed and without a job. This turned out to be a blessing in disguise as now I was able to attend many of the events at the Olympic Games. I lived in humble digs in Carramar near the then-notorious Cabramatta, and found myself elected to an Olympic Games committee for the City of Fairfield. The experiences gained in my travels around Australia and living and ministering in the south-west of Sydney helped me immensely for what God had prepared for me back home in the Upper Yarra Valley.

I returned to Warburton fit and invigorated and ready to bring Peter home. My heart was in the right place when I chose to bring him to live with me and possibly to die. When I collected him from the nursing home in Healesville, all of his worldly possessions were contained in one plastic bag. There were worn and torn flannelette pyjamas, a toothbrush and toothpaste, a spare set of dentures, a few papers, an address book and his passport. The clothes he was wearing were tattered and well past their use-by date, which was a pitiful sight. I prepared his bedroom that overlooked a majestic semi-tropical rainforest, and when he'd had a decent rest I drove him to the Yarra Junction Opportunity Shop where at no charge he was suitably outfitted by their compassionate manager.

By now Peter had virtually no conversation and would have to think for a long time before he could answer even the simplest question. He appeared to be mesmerised, as though he was having a conversation inside his head with his best friend! My vast Christian experience now showed me clearly that he was being severely demonised.*

When I look back at this scene, I realise I was playing the role not only of big brother but also of Mum and Dad. One may conclude I had a martyr complex,* but no, this was all part of God's plan.

I could go on and on about what happened for the next few weeks. I prepared nutritious meals but Peter wouldn't eat them; instead, he'd raid the refrigerator during the night and drink the bottle of milk straight from the bottle and leave the empty bottle in the refrigerator door. Meals On Wheels provided a break from cooking for me, but he wouldn't touch their food. He didn't want to wash and I couldn't see myself showering him, so through the Shire of Yarra Ranges I was able to arrange for a nurse to bathe him. This quickly became too much for one person so two nurses had to be sent.

One night when I was sound asleep I was awakened in fright by a noise next to my bed. Here was Peter standing over me with a glazed look in his eyes that really frightened me. Was I in danger for my life? I was now getting frantic – *I must escape this depressing scene before I go mad!* (I was used to escaping from our family home years ago when our mother fell into the pit of depression.)

On my knees in desperation I once again prayed that God would give me a short break, and before I knew it I found myself making an appointment with the manager of Pallotti College in Millgrove which was established many years ago as a Roman Catholic retreat[1] but was now open to people from all Christian denominations. I was desperate for carer respite, but after the unburdening of my tale of woe with the manager, none of the compassion I'd expected from a man of God was shown. He replied dismissively, 'I'm sorry, Mr Penman. We can't help you. You'll have to look elsewhere.'

Righteous anger flared up within me – I was furious but kept my cool and replied unambiguously, 'What would Jesus do?'

The next day Peter became a paying guest at the retreat house on the property called Casa Pallotti. With a retired priest and his elderly, compassionate female carer, here Peter remained while I took a two weeks' sabbatical at Mission Beach in Queensland to recover my sanity and to earnestly pray.

So far, I've painted a bleak picture of my sojourn in the Upper Yarra Valley but not all was black. On Thursdays and Saturdays I played competitive tennis in North Ringwood, a long way to travel but necessary to find strong competition. On Wednesday afternoons I joined a small group of my friends playing the card game known as Solo in alternating private homes around Warburton, which was always a pleasant escape. After church on Sundays a group of us could be found unwinding over lunch at one of the fine cafés in the main street of Warburton and afterwards leisurely strolling along the banks of the Yarra. You could find me on Sunday afternoons bopping away to the trad jazz music played by Neville Turner's band, Four Bars In,[2] at the Alpine Retreat Hotel in the main street.

There were a couple of romantic interludes along the way, one of which sadly was to end in tragedy.

1 Society of the Catholic Apostolate: Pallottine Fathers and Brothers – Australian Region.
2 Neville and I became good friends at St Mary's Church, at tennis and playing Solo.

CHAPTER 21

A DISASTER WAITING
TO HAPPEN

R evived and revitalised by my respite at Mission Beach, I
returned to Warburton ready to continue my journey with
Peter. When I left Peter at Pallotti I'd withdrawn all his prescribed
medications and had substituted placebos in the form of multivi-
tamin tablets and capsules. Peter was fed wholesome home-cooked
meals at Pallotti, and their report when I picked him up was that
he'd been quiet, kept to himself much of the time and was co-
operative, especially when it was time to dry the dishes. He'd been
tenderly cared for in a homely environment by two precious
people of God and, bringing him home from Pallotti in better
health, I embarked on a plan to get him well again, or so I
thought.

It's intriguing living with a person with a mental disability –
you tend to watch their every move, not in a voyeuristic way but
so you can monitor their progress or regress. What was disturbing
me most was Peter's toileting habits; he wasn't going to the toilet

and was beginning to get bloated, so much so that I made an appointment with the Warburton Medical Clinic where he was prescribed a shifting formula, which simply didn't work. I tried to get Peter to exercise but this was impossible: he'd walk a few steps to the front gate and just stand there with that vacant look, staring into the vast unknown. As each day passed, things got worse and soon he became aggressive to the point of violence. I couldn't get him into the car – he would lash out at me – not verbally but physically, so in desperation I phoned the emergency number 000 and asked to be put through to the ambulance, explaining the situation as best I could. They were extremely busy as there'd been a fatal car crash along the highway at Wandin, so understandably the officer said, 'Can't you bring your brother to the hospital in your car? They'll give him a good clean-out.'

I had to reply, 'I can't get him into the car. He keeps fighting me off.'

The officer agreed reluctantly to send an ambulance and, with quite a deal of resistance, Peter was taken to the Outpatients Department at the Maroondah Hospital in Ringwood. By now I was so tired I didn't have the energy to accompany him or to follow in my car. I was emotionally drained and physically exhausted as by now all of my reserves had been depleted. I'd finally come to the end of my tether. Had I made a huge mistake by bringing Peter home? No, I hadn't. I'd done my very best in these most difficult circumstances.

While all of this was happening, behind the scenes I'd being praying about the possibility of returning to Melbourne as I'd been in the Upper Yarra Valley for seven years and had a sense that the season there was coming to an end. I'd heard about an Anglican Church property through my good Christian friend John who had recently moved there from Frankston. He was so happy in his new home unit close to the Chadstone Shopping Centre and near public transport, so when John invited me to come down and see it I didn't hesitate to drive down from Warburton. After a tour of the property I was so impressed I made immediate enquiries about moving there.

CHAPTER 22

CHRISTIAN MINISTRY AT THE COALFACE

Don't think it's easy writing a book like this! My sleep patterns are disturbed as I'm drawn deeper into the writing abyss. Some say I often wander off the beaten track when I'm writing and I do. Others say I go walkabout and I do. I make no apology for another bend in the road, an unintended consequence of delving so deeply into my brain's vast deposits. There's so much to get off my chest.

This chapter is devoted to my role as a lay Christian minister and has nothing to do with my brother.

The word *minister* is derived from the Latin word for 'to serve' or 'to be a servant'. Research shows that men and women ordained as ministers by the Church account for a mere 5% of people. The rest are lay people like me and possibly like some of you, called by God to serve and not to be served. This chapter therefore acts as an interlude or a bridge before I cross over into much more rugged terrain.

On the steps of Saint Mary's Warburton

You'd think my frenetic lifestyle in Warburton, outlined already, precluded me from spending time in the presence of God.[1] Not so. Much of my time alone was spent in silent prayer, occasional fasting, meditation and contemplation. My home overlooking the semi-tropical rainforest became the perfect war room[2] where I was to confront many demons in spiritual warfare.* There was rarely time for television and little time for radio. I discarded the mobile phone and cut off all social media and, when not praying alone, prayed with partners around Melbourne and by phone beyond.

Formal ministry happened at St Mary's where I was responsible for the food bank and had the vision to establish a ministry to men which I called Blokes' Brunch. From time to time I was called upon by our ordained minister, the Reverend Gail

Pinchbeck,[3] to accompany her as she ministered in difficult and sometimes threatening circumstances. I also became a volunteer driver with LinC (Love in the Name of Christ, a well-known and respected ministry in the Upper Yarra Valley), but by far the bulk of the ministry God called me to was on my own – and highly unusual to say the least.

The population at large sees the role of a minister or priest (or rabbi) as the person out in front on Sundays (or Saturdays), often wearing an unusual dress! On other days of the week he or she will be officiating at funerals or even at a wedding, a ceremony which is fast becoming a relic of the past. This is called public ministry, the ministry you and I see. Private ministry by ordained ministers or lay people like me, and possibly you, is vastly different. Let me give you some insight.

Meet ALAN. My neighbour in the dilapidated house across the road used to shine his outside light straight into my kitchen window. One night I caught him peering through the window. He's a Peeping Tom. I gave this voyeur the rounds of the kitchen and sent him off with his tail between his legs and then reported him to the local police. One night some weeks later, when I was waiting on the dirt road outside my place to be picked up to be driven to a meeting, I saw Alan through their lounge-room window masturbating in front of his twelve-year-old daughter. I immediately reported this incident as well. A couple of months later I heard on the grapevine that his daughter was pregnant to him, and the last I heard about Alan was that he was serving time in prison.

Meet KEITH. I met Keith through Centrelink in Yarra Junction. I'd established the ministry to men and was looking to befriend the many men marginalised by society who might need a sincere, non-judgmental mate. Their manager suggested I contact one of their customers who was in a really bad way and could do with a decent friend. This is what I wrote when I first met Keith:

> It was cold for an early April morning, early autumn in this part of the world. We were in the Upper Yarra Valley where snow falls early on the nearby Donna Buang mountain so the chill wind shouldn't be unexpected. Keith stood awkwardly against the doorway of the Opportunity Shop, a man about my age then – in his late fifties. His grey beard was matched by his pallid complexion, offset by a heavily wrinkled brow. I guess he would've been about 5 feet 10 inches tall. His jeans were unkempt, his T-shirt rumpled and ragged. He was hunched up, haggard, and gazed nonchalantly at the passing parade. Observing this man from a discreet distance hidden from view under a bus shelter, I realised this man must be Keith. I introduced myself and listened to this sad story.
>
> Keith was living in deep depression at the Doon Reserve Caravan Park in Yarra Junction. His wife of over twenty years had run off with a high-flyer from the Fairfax media who was in a long-term same-sex relationship but due to societal norms at the time hadn't come out. At public functions he solicited Keith's wife to be his escort to disguise his true self. One day Keith returned home to find his home stripped bare of all the possessions he and his wife had accumulated over the fifteen years of their marriage. She had been invited to be the Fairfax bloke's partner, which she had accepted. Keith was left bewildered and devastated and broke, and lapsed into this deep depression.

As a consequence of this desertion Keith chose to hide away in his unkempt caravan with a few meagre possessions and windows draped with heavy dark curtains. He was addicted to the caffeine in coffee and to the nicotine in tobacco. Keith smoked 'chop-chop' – illegal, roll-your-own, cheap cigarettes – as though they were going out of fashion! The stench in the caravan was overwhelming.

For more than five years I visited Keith regularly and at my suggestion he volunteered to mow the lawns at the Anglican Church property in Yarra Junction with a petrol mower I'd donated. One day he cut off one of his toes and when I visited him later in Box Hill Hospital he quipped, 'That's life, mate.'

Keith became a volunteer with Blokes' Brunch and was so excited when he heard I'd invited John Schultz, 'The Rucking Giant' and my competition tennis partner and Footscray's 1960 Brownlow Medallist, to be guest speaker, as he was one of Keith's footy idols.

In time, after much encouragement by me, Keith quit his addiction to cigarettes and reduced his coffee intake to a minimum. After a lot of effort I was able to get him to see the community dentist where dentures were duly fitted, and with a lot of pushing and shoving I was able to encourage Keith to apply for public housing; in due course he was offered and accepted a unit in Tecoma where he resides today. What has happened to Keith since is a story only he can tell as I've lost contact with him.

Meet JAMES. My neighbour on one side of me was a young man called James. His wife had recently divorced him due to his addiction to alcohol and the physical abuse that ensued. We would meet most mornings for breakfast at either his place or mine where we would read and study the Bible and over time I led James to the Lord and duly baptised him by full immersion in the Yarra River, assisted by Keith. Afterwards James sold his house and moved to England. Some months later he phoned me from the UK in an alcoholic stupor. And that's the last I've heard of him.

Meet BLAIR. James's house was purchased by Blair, another alcoholic, who said to me one day, 'Now that I'm taking tablets for my depression I'm only drinking eight stubbies of a night.'

One freezing winter's night (and it can drop to below zero where I was living), there was a *bang, bang* on my back door. It was Blair, totally off his face with booze. He'd been with his drunken mates at the local fish farm off the Warburton Highway. Blair couldn't find his car keys, let alone his car, so he wandered barefoot up the steep hill and through the bush to finally land at my dining-room door.

A dinky-die Irishman, he reeked of whiskey and was smashed to the back teeth. I rushed to the laundry and grabbed an empty bucket just in time to catch the gush of vomit surging from deep within. I left him there and went to bed and I'm so thankful to God that Blair was nowhere to be seen the next morning, or for days afterwards.

Meet JASON. There were all sorts of problems at the Warburton Tennis Club. A group of *ballsy* women wanted to take control of the committee, and reluctantly it was decided they were to have their way. They connived to appoint a fall guy in my place as president and quickly appointed a tennis coach who for some time had been casing the joint. I had a really bad feeling about this bloke and it was confirmed when a mother of one of the young girls I'd been coaching said, 'Paul. The new coach wants to teach my daughter privately. What do you think?'

I had to think very carefully before I replied, 'I wouldn't agree to it if I were you.'

I was in prayer soon afterwards and felt the compulsion to phone Tennis Australia and to speak to the then Chief Executive Steve Wood, whom I knew personally. This is how the conversation went:

'Steve, I'm concerned about the new coach who's been appointed at the Warburton Tennis Club. Do you know anything about him?'

The pause was deafening.

'Paul, we've been trailing Jason for the last four weeks. He's now in jail.'

Meet BAZZA. Caravan parks are a lifeline for some permanent residents in Victoria but are considered one step away from homelessness. One woman I regularly bumped into around Warburton who lived in the Warburton Caravan Park had such low self-esteem she called herself trailer-trash. *How sad*, I thought. One particular caravan park in the Upper Yarra Valley is well known for being the place to keep up your supply of illegal drugs once you've been released from prison. This is where Bazza was to be found. One day at Blokes' Brunch this gentle giant appeared at the church hall door with the opening words, 'Got a beer, mate?'

I was quick to reply, 'Sorry, mate. We're not an "early opener". How about a coffee or a cuppa?'

Bazza was fifty, fat and anxious, but once he'd settled down and started to trust us he began to relax. 'Yer know, mate, I've just got out of jail. Gees it's hard outside, mate! I'm going to re-offend 'cause things have changed so much since I was inside I can't cope no more.'

Bazza gulped down his meal and headed for I-don't-know-where.

Meet BONNIE & CLYDE. Last but by no means least, here's another true story from the pages of my now almost obliterated memory. The story is concerned with – let's call them Bonnie & Clyde – not their real names of course. This married Kiwi couple in their early thirties hailed from the North Island of New Zealand, and when Clyde first appeared at Blokes' Brunch he and Bonnie were living in a two-man tent by the Yarra River in the Warburton Caravan Park. Feeling compassion for them immediately, I began a routine of baking a loaf of bread for them which I'd deliver to the caravan park most mornings. In time they shared their journey with me, a story just too sad to be told. Childless and penniless, Clyde had spent some years in Her Majesty's Prison in New Zealand on a charge of attempted murder, and after he'd been released Bonnie tagged along beside him. They worked together on local farms and in the vineyards throughout the Yarra Valley, finding whatever work they could from season to season. They could often be seen walking side by side, thumbing a lift from the passing cars on the Warburton Highway.

I only once managed to get them to come to church, but after Bonnie had a work-related accident and could now only hobble they liked to stay home on Sundays and rest, which made sense to me.

They befriended my next-door neighbour, and one Saturday night, judging by the noise coming from the house next door, it was obvious there was a drunken sexual orgy taking place. Very late that night there was to be yet another drunken man at my back door. This time it was Clyde.

Apparently there'd been an argument over whose turn it was to have sex with Bonnie! Clyde was too drunk to care and had decided to come over to his friend Paul's place for consolation and his first drunken words to me were indelicately delivered thus: 'How about a f—?'

To which I quickly replied, seeing the obvious ridiculousness of the situation, 'No thanks. I'm not that sort of girl!'

With a glazed look in his half-shut eyes Clyde slumped into the chair that Blair had spewed from.

I followed up my refusal of his ludicrous proposal with, 'There's a single bed in that bedroom up the corridor. How about sleeping there tonight? You can try to sort out the problems with your wife tomorrow.'

He slouched off and fell rejected onto the bed, but not before concealing something under the mattress.

In the morning he was gone. I looked under the mattress and there was an opened flick-knife. I worked out that here was Clyde's protection against being assaulted or raped during the long and lonely night-time hours in prison.

Weeks passed. I saw neither sight nor sound of Bonnie & Clyde until, one day, there they were, with sacks on their backs on the road again.

Now it's time once again to return to my journey with Peter.

---

1 When you read and absorb what follows you'll wonder how I ever had the resilience and time to become involved with these people and situations. God gave me supernatural energy for the task.

2 The 2015 movie *War Room*: 'The most slickly produced and insistently evangelic movie' – *Variety Magazine*. This US film, produced by brothers Alex and Stephen Kendrick, is all about warfare praying by mature Christians.

3 Now elevated to Archdeacon.

CHAPTER 23

PAUL – YOU'VE ABANDONED YOUR BROTHER!

I take my hat off to all the 'ambos' and paramedics out there and to all the staff working in hospital emergency wards. What an enormous self-sacrificing contribution you're making to our society.

There was Peter the next morning being flushed out by a nurse on a bed in the emergency unit. The stench must have been overpowering. He acknowledged me with a half-smile as I sought out the social worker on duty, who turned out to be a young, pretty and dedicated professional, and sensitive to my outpouring of grief as I told her what had been happening for the past few weeks: 'I don't know what to do with him now. I can't bring him home with me or I'll be the one having a nervous breakdown. Please, please, help me.'

She thought for a few moments. 'Mr Penman, please wait here while I speak with my supervisor.'

Turning, then disappearing around a corner, she returned about ten minutes later. 'I've discussed your brother with my supervisor and we believe the best course of action is to find Peter a nursing home somewhere close to where you live.'

'But he's no money.'

'That's all right. We'll find him a place subsidised by the government. There are a limited number of beds made available for people on a disability pension.'

She then produced a list of nursing homes where there appeared to be vacancies. I replied, 'I expect to be returning to Melbourne shorty. Could there be any beds close to Chadstone?'

She scanned the list and highlighted a nursing home in East Oakleigh, which wasn't too far from Chadstone, and after a couple of days in West Ward at Maroondah Hospital, Peter was transported by ambulance to Oakmoor Nursing Home in Warrigal Road. At last I could breathe a sigh of relief.

It was 2005 when my name appeared on the top of the waiting list for a church property near Chadstone, so I moved from Warburton and was soon settled into a new world back in suburbia.

It wasn't long before a letter arrived in the mail in an official-looking envelope. I'd been summonsed to appear at the Ringwood Magistrates' Court, accused of abandoning my brother at the Maroondah Hospital. The day of the hearing arrived and I pleaded my case to the magistrate, who could easily identify with my predicament with Peter. The summons was withdrawn and I cried.

CHAPTER 24

THE TROUBLE IS, PAUL –
I KNOW I'M MAD

Peter at Oakmoor

I'd driven past Oakmoor many times over the years and I'd said to myself I'd never want to have to be put in there. And here was Peter, my beloved brother, moving into this hellhole and returning to the medication Cocktail Hour regime, served some of the time by unqualified staff. Prescribing doctors and diligent dispensers, don't get me wrong. Drugs have their place, but it's hard when the only words your brother says after being off them for a number of weeks and now back on them are, 'The trouble is, Paul – I know I'm mad.'

And on the next visit a few days later, 'I'm living in a black hole and I can't get out.'

And the following day, 'I'm dead. I'm dead. Paul, I'm dead.'

Peter was stuck in a room at the end of the building along with a couple of other victims. There were no outside areas to capture sunlight, and the atmosphere was so depressing that you'd be better off shooting yourself than having to put up with being so demoralised in this prison-like hellhole.

Having had years of experience visiting my mother in such places, I'd become expert at calling in to see Peter at odd times, especially out of normal visiting hours, just to see what was going on. Like most of these places Oakmoor was short-staffed (you could always tell by the pungent smell of urine) with workers run off their feet and owned by greedy entrepreneurs wanting to make a fast buck.

At one stage it was obvious Peter was having trouble with his dentures. His gums were ulcerated so he wouldn't wear them. I'd asked for the Royal Dental Hospital to be contacted weeks beforehand and was assured that this had been done. One day in frustration when nothing was happening, when visiting Peter I boldly picked up their phone and spoke to the appointments department at the dental hospital.

'Peter who? We have no record of a Peter Penman.'

Did I see red and did I let them have it! Two days later there was a visit by a dentist from the Royal Melbourne Dental Hospital and straight away Peter's false teeth fitted perfectly.[1]

Shortly after Peter arrived at Oakmoor, I happened to glance at their notice board to read that this facility was soon to be closed down. (Thank you, God!) Residents would be progressively moved to Elanora, a superior facility located in fashionable Brighton. Hallelujah. There's hope at last.

---

1 This gives me the perfect opportunity to thank the Royal Dental Hospital of Melbourne. I have been a patient of theirs for many years due to my cleft lip and palate and I couldn't speak more highly of them.

CHAPTER 25

BEAUTIFUL BRIGHTON
BY THE BAY

As soon as I read the notice I hotfooted it down to Brighton and was warmly greeted by a mature, well-dressed woman in her early forties who was more than happy to show me through the expansive buildings which were being substantially renovated and extended. The place was like a gilded cage – so luxurious, imposing and obviously premium residential care for families who could afford the fees. After the tour was over, my guide concluded, 'Mr Penman, it has been a pleasure showing you around as we are so proud of what we offer here. Be assured we'll look after your brother and I'll personally see to it that Peter will be one of the first to be relocated from Oakmoor.'

Am I dreaming? Am I hearing things? At last my brother was being treated like a human being. In early 2006 and true to her word, Peter was transferred to Elanora.

I have so many happy memories of Brighton. As already written we were married at St Andrew's in Middle Brighton and when we first came to live in Melbourne we boarded with my wife's parents in East Brighton. Elanora was only a stone's throw from the bay and in walking distance to Milano's on the Esplanade, our family's favourite Italian bistro.[1] Oh what bliss as seagulls serenaded as they flew nearby and lovers walked hand in hand along the promenade. As cyclists flashed their fashionable luminous Lycra as they rode by, I thanked the Lord for His unmerited favour and pondered if this would be Peter's final resting place. 'Gracious Lord, thank You. Thank You. Thank You. Is anything impossible for You?'

My visits to Peter became less regular once he'd settled in because I was confident he was at last being well cared for. My children and grandchildren visited him from time to time, especially when the annual Christmas party was held and Santa arrived. Soon all the family remarked at what an improvement Elanora was after the bedlam at Oakmoor. But in spite of his new surroundings and the extra care, Peter's condition continued to deteriorate and this is what I wrote at the time:

> I arrived late in the afternoon to find Peter in the 'play' room. The young Sri Lankan nurse's aide was supervising a balloon game with the patients arranged in a circle in their chairs and wheelchairs. Today Peter was pleased to see me as I told him I was planning a trip to his former stamping ground in south-east Queensland. We talked about golf, a subject that keeps his interest, if only momentarily. After about five minutes Peter was anxious for me to leave and said, 'It's four o'clock. They come and put me to bed now.'

Peter had to be admitted to the nearby Sandringham Hospital on three occasions and each time it was up to me to arrange the move there and back. At 1 a.m. on one occasion my phone rang.

'Hello, is that Paul? It's Margaret, the night nurse at Elanora calling. I have a doctor on the phone who wishes to speak with you.'

'Hello, Paul. I'm the locum here. I've been called out by the nursing home about your brother. Peter is not at all well and we want to send him to hospital. Can we have your permission?'[2]

Peter was having problems breathing again, but that pales into insignificance compared with what followed.

1 In those days it was called Mario's.
2 I was Peter's Medical Power of Attorney.

CHAPTER 26

THE DRUG OF LAST RESORT

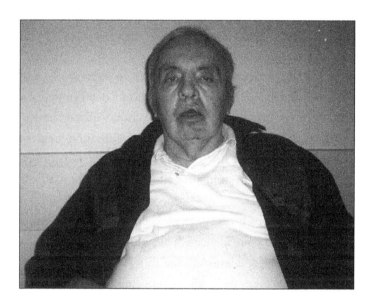

It was at about this time that Peter's general practitioner and consultant psychiatrist collaborated to come to a decision that something drastic had to be tried in the hope of stabilising Peter's mental condition. Every drug they'd prescribed hadn't had the effect they'd anticipated, every attempt at occupational therapy had little success, and the frequent sessions of electroconvulsive

89

therapy had made absolutely no difference. In their collective wisdom there remained only one option, to prescribe Clozapine, a drug known as 'the drug of last resort'.

When asked to give my permission for Peter to be administered this drug, I immediately went to my family to discuss this drastic option. No-one was prepared to make a decision so I decided that if this was to be the cure, let's take a chance. So I prayed.[1] It was a risky business taking this drug as it was so potent that permission to prescribe it, like many other drugs, had to come from the Department of Health in Canberra, and because of its toxicity and potential side-effects a blood test had to be given every week.

After trialling this potent drug on Peter for some weeks, there was no visible change; in fact his condition deteriorated even further to the point where he had a psychotic episode and was admitted to the Kingston Community Rehabilitation Centre in Cheltenham. Soon after he was admitted a night nurse caught Peter just in time to prevent him from throwing himself off a first-floor balcony.[2]

Writers are Bower birds – we pick up things all the time – therefore it was no coincidence when writing this chapter that I came across a newspaper article: 'The Pain Killers: What happens when the cure becomes the cause of almost unbearable suffering?' This article[3] about the overuse of opioids, medications that relieve pain, has some alarming things to say about other drugs. Some edited extracts follow.

> In Victoria, where more people die each year from pharmaceutical overdoses than road accidents, Coroner's Court data for 2009 to 2015 underscores the complexity of the issue; the anti-anxiety benzodiazepine group of drugs (most

prominently, the pernicious diazepam, or Valium) contributed to more deaths than opioids. Most overdose deaths involved multiple drugs, most typically, opioids and benzos, often with alcohol …

In June 2014, three young Sydneysiders who had not crossed paths in life became posthumously united when the NSW coroner delivered simultaneous findings into their deaths. Christopher Salib was 24 when he died on February 6, 2011, at his Eastlakes home. Salib, once an award-winning apprentice car mechanic, was found to have toxic levels of codeine, oxycodone and the antidepressant Paroxetine in his blood. Shamsad Akhtar died on June 6, 2011, at her Plumpton home. She was 35. Her three young children were near her when she died. In the last 11 days of her life she was prescribed antidepressants, sleep aids, benzodiazepines and pain killers including codeine. Nathan Attard, a former carpenter, was 34 when his body was found in his Redfern unit on March 24, 2012. Police found empty packets of morphine, diazepam and the antidepressant Mirtazapine; an autopsy found he had toxic levels of Mirtazapine and codeine in his liver.

Each had a different, troubled story but the then-deputy state coroner Carmel Forbes' conclusion was the same. 'Multidrug toxicity' was a cause or contributing cause in each death. (Opioids, especially when used with other drugs, can depress a person's central nervous system, leading to respiratory failure.) 'There is little doubt that the misuse and abuse of addictive prescription medication is a serious public health issue … This inquest has illustrated that all manner of unfortunate people are getting caught up with addictive prescription medication,' the coroner said …

In Victoria, Dr Matthew Frei, the head of clinical services for the Turning Point Alcohol and Drug Centre in Melbourne's Eastern Health region [said] ... 'Let's just own this: we're drugging a huge swathe of the population ... So often these medications are just a panacea, used to treat everything from loneliness to insomnia to sadness to anxiety. That's just the history of these drugs.'

1 'Praise be to God, who has not rejected my prayer' (Psalm 66:20).
2 This product works for many patients but it certainly didn't work for Peter.
3 'Good Weekend', *The Age* (Melbourne), 4 June 2016.

CHAPTER 27

SUPERNATURAL INTERVENTION

I t *seems there's no longer hope for Peter. Nearly fifty years have passed since that first breakdown and where are we now?* These are my gloomy thoughts as I sit in front of my heater on this wet and miserable Sunday afternoon in early winter. I look up to the foreboding sky, perhaps an omen for what's ahead, and acknowledge that my help can now come only from the Lord,[1] and as I reach into my record collection and play Handel's sacred oratorio *Messiah*, these words ring out:

> Surely He hath borne our griefs, and carried our sorrows!
> He was wounded for our transgressions; He was bruised
> for our iniquities;
> the chastisement of our peace was upon Him.
> And with His stripes we are healed.[2]

Then the words of sacred music we sang when I was a choirboy resonated:

I waited for the Lord, he inclined unto me,

He heard my complaint, he heard my complaint.[3]

Then it struck me! Why hadn't I thought of this before? *I must make an appointment with the Pastoral Lay Minister at St Paul's in North Caulfield. This humble man has been anointed* by God to intercede* on Peter's behalf.*

The appointment made, I'm now in his office, his war room. After running through the history of Peter's journey, our Pastoral Lay Minister prays, then remarks, 'I don't know how your brother is still alive considering all the spiritual attacks that have come against him.' He deliberates for a while and adds, 'What we'll do is get you to "stand in the gap"* for Peter... in other words to intercede on Peter's behalf. I'll pray and you'll be substituting for Peter.'

Then follows extended praying as he beseeches our Lord to intervene in this frightful situation. He continues praying for at least ten minutes as I stand in the gap for Peter. At the end of his prayers he concludes, 'It was sensible of you to ask to stand in the gap for Peter. If we had prayed for him at the nursing home he would most likely have manifested* and the nursing staff wouldn't know what was going on and consequently what to do... It will possibly take up to a year to see the results of our prayers, but in time there will be positive results. Nothing is impossible with God.'

I continued to visit Peter regularly and he gradually became more sociable. There were no sudden outbursts and he seemed to be more relaxed. He was actually pleased to see me! I said nothing to the staff about Peter's deliverance ministry,* knowing full well that such a subject would be off limits. They also might have thought I was the madman and attempt to admit me!

During Peter's time at Elanora there were two more short stays at the Sandringham Hospital. On one occasion he'd developed pneumonia and the other was caused by more breathing difficulties and I wondered at the time if this had anything to do with the medications he was ingesting. By now I was feeling exhausted. In the past I'd arranged to transport Peter to and from the hospital but now this was getting beyond me. My capacity to do more than I was doing was being rapidly depleted.

1 'I lift my eyes to the hills – where does my help come from? My help comes from the LORD, the Maker of heaven and earth' (Psalm 121:1–2).
2 'He was despised and rejected by men, a man of sorrows, and familiar with suffering. Like one from whom men hide their faces he was despised, and we esteemed him not. Surely he took up our infirmities and carried our sorrows, yet we consider him stricken by God, smitten by him, and afflicted. But he was pierced for our transgressions, he was crushed for our iniquities; the punishment that brought us peace was upon him, and by his wounds we are healed' (Isaiah 53:3–5). (As I read this I began to weep.)
3 Mendelssohn (1809–1847), 'Hymn of Praise', Cantata, Symphony No. 2, Opus 52.

CHAPTER 28

WANDERING THE KING'S HIGHWAY

I'm old-fashioned and enjoy listening to old-fashioned music on my old-fashioned gramophone. I'm also getting very tired. The responsibility for looking after Peter is getting me down, so as I listen to a 1948 recording of Peter Dawson singing 'Wandering the King's Highway', I'm moved by the following lyrics:

> I've always been a wanderer,
> summer and winter too.
> Travelling the whole world over,
> tramping my whole life through.
> But when I start my journey,
> at the dawn of another day,
> I give a health to comrades,
> Friends of the great highway.
>
> *Chorus*:
> So, so long to you!
> Got to be on the road again.

So long to you!
Got to hitch up my load again.
It's been great to meet you here,
right good company and right good cheer.
So now then, my lads,
would anyone like to come with me?
A wanderer's life is free.

Lyrics: L. Coward

These words could well have been written especially for Peter, but today I sense they're for me – I'm to go wandering – to revisit most of the places Peter lived. I've a premonition that Peter isn't going to be with us for much longer so I pack my bags and head north. It's the end of July 2011 and my plan is to be away for about three weeks.

I fly to Coolangatta and spend a few days catching up with old friends Kevin and Marilyn, bunking down in their caravan in Kingscliff. I bus and train it to Brisbane where I hire a car and head for Noosa where I stay for a few days and have a well-earned rest. Then I head off for Ipswich and criss-cross to Buderim, Mooloolaba,[1] Gatton, Warwick,[2] Oakey, Esk, Crow's Nest, Goombungee and Toowoomba. What amazed me on this trip was that Peter always squatted near a golf course. He may have lost his marbles but he still settled near a golf club so as to hit the occasional golf ball.

1 Representing Manly Surf Life-Saving Club, Peter competed in the Australian Surf Life-Saving Championships at the Mooloolaba Surf Club in the late 1950s. When I visited their luxurious club I had the seafood platter (Mooloola derives from the Aboriginal word *mulu*, meaning snapper fish). Be sure not to miss it!
2 I sank a couple of stubbies on the banks of the Condamine River.

CHAPTER 29

CLOSE TO HOME
AND FAMILY

Over the next twelve months Peter's overall health gradually began to improve. Signs were now obvious that the deliverance ministry was taking effect, but there were now physical issues to contend with. Sadly at this time my former wife was diagnosed with Alzheimer's disease so our daughters began to investigate more appropriate living arrangements for her. They hit upon a place called Oak Towers in Oakleigh, located directly opposite the home unit I'd purchased after the dissolution of our marriage years before. It was premature to move her as her condition was such that there still remained time to live independently, so a quaint home unit was secured on a property owned by Oak Towers in nearby Grant Street. I had no problems with the way Peter was being cared for at Elanora, but Brighton was quite a distance to travel and from a practical perspective Oak Towers struck a chord with me. It was in walking distance from where I lived and not far from one of my daughters who lived just down the road, so I made enquiries about relocating Peter there. As it happened[1] a government-subsidised bed had just become available in their high-care section so Peter was transferred from Elanora by ambulance in March 2012.

For some time Peter had been complaining about pain in his stomach and occasional pains in his lower back. I mentioned this to his doctor who suggested Peter be thoroughly checked over, so I arranged medical transport and accompanied him to the Monash Medical Centre in nearby Clayton. We arrived at the Outpatients Department at 9 a.m. and were still sitting there at 8 p.m. It took a number of protestations with staff to finally get Peter looked at, and at 9 p.m. he was admitted and stayed there overnight. After a multitude of tests a large growth was discovered,[2] the consensus of opinion being that this was inoperable. My premonition was fast becoming a reality.

1 Some say this was a coincidence; others say I was lucky. It was neither – it was a God incident, not a coincidence.
2 Bowel cancer.

CHAPTER 30

WHY IS PETER IN
HIGH CARE?

It was just marvellous having Peter living so close. I could visit him more often. My younger daughter and her boys called in to see Peter frequently and one day I met a man called Alan who was a volunteer visiting the patients. I met Alan in the High Dependency Unit soon after Peter was admitted. Alan's wife had died here and in his words he was there because, 'I wanted to give something back to those who'd cared for my wife so compassionately.'

Unbeknown to me, Alan and Peter had become good mates.

Months went by and the improvement in Peter's mental capabilities was quite remarkable and a joy to behold. Sometimes he made me really laugh! He was usually to be found in the large living room overlooking the courtyard garden, or he'd be watching television or playing games supervised by an occupational therapist. At last Peter would be pleased to see me, unlike the old days when he used to debase me by saying, 'What are *you* doing here?'

Things were completely different now. Instead of looking at me like his worst enemy, he'd greet me as his concerned little brother. Now his conversation was always lucid and we had chats about the family, mutual friends, sport, and of course the Melbourne weather, always something to talk about. One day after one of the young nurses walked past, he amused me when under his breath he said, 'Hasn't she got a big bottom!'

Other comments like this amused me too. For example, he'd look me up and down and say, 'Paul – you're putting on weight [you're getting fat]' or 'Paul – you need a haircut.'

Yes. My prayers had been answered – I'd got my big brother back. Thank you, Lord.

People may conclude that Peter's amazingly improved mental state was due to the fact he was now receiving more regular visits from the family and that his new surroundings, staff and routine were playing a more positive role, but the reality was quite different. Oak Towers was no better than Elanora had been. The environment was similar and his medication remained the same. Peter was visibly different and everyone agreed. There was no doubt about it – Peter was a changed man.

Let's now return to Alan, Peter's new best friend.

As it happened Alan and I both belonged to the Chadstone Tennis Club, a local club where we played in a men's social group during the week. One morning when some of us were sitting around having a cup of tea between sets, Alan piped up and right out of the blue said, 'I used to read to Peter. Did you know he had an interest in the stock exchange?' Alan thought for a moment, then added, 'Peter was quite normal, not like the other residents there. I used to enjoy our conversations. Peter was a real gentleman; I don't know why they had him in the high-care unit.'

CHAPTER 31

HE WAS POTTING PETUNIAS

It was late spring when I was in my courtyard garden, potting petunias and thinking about Peter. He'd now settled into Oak Towers and, other than the physical diagnosis, we didn't talk about how he was mentally and emotionally well and appreciated the many jokes I'd try to humour him with, especially the Irish ones. It was so encouraging seeing him laugh when I ran a new joke past him.

Taking a break from gardening I went inside to have a rest and, as I did so, gained the distinct impression I had to call in to see Peter. So after a 'grandpa nap' I showered, dressed and drove to Oak Towers to find him with other patients and nurses, also potting petunias in the courtyard garden.

On this bright, sunny Melbourne afternoon we spent over an hour enjoying quality time together, conversing and laughing with the other patients and the nurses about all sorts of trivia, including how coincidental[1] it was that I'd also been potting petunias in my courtyard garden. When it was cleaning-up time Peter looked at me and said (more like instructed me, like big brothers do), 'Take my hat back to my room, will you!'

I was so glad he talked like the good old days. Yes, big brother was telling little brother what to do.

After leaving Peter's hat in his room I returned to the garden and Peter was nowhere to be seen, so I left with a bounce in my step and joy in my heart. It must have been about three o'clock.

1 It was not a coincidence!

CHAPTER 32

THE END OF PETER'S EARTHLY JOURNEY

It was about 5.30 that afternoon when the phone rang.

'Is that Paul? It's the sister in charge at Oak Towers. I'm very sorry to have to tell you that your brother has passed away.'

Just exactly what happened after that is just a blur as I can't remember much about it now. All I can remember is I phoned my daughter, gave her the news and burst into tears.

'Will you come with me to see Peter?'

'Of course I will, Dad; I'll be at your place in fifteen minutes.'

We were told that Peter had just finished his evening meal in the dining room when he got up from the table and slumped, staggered, then fell to the floor and died. The fatal heart attack took just eleven seconds and now it was all over.

When we arrived Peter looked so peaceful as he lay there on his bed in his room. I went to his side, stroked his forehead and kissed him tenderly on the cheek, saying, 'See yer later, mate.'

I knew I would see him again.

My daughter and I both cried, and we left inconsolably.

I'd prepaid Peter's funeral some years before, using funds held with the Public Trustees. The funeral was held at St Mary's in Warburton and conducted by our dear friend Gail Pinchbeck, who for some years had travelled with me on this journey. I composed the eulogy in tears, but because I was so distraught couldn't face having to get up on the podium in front of people to deliver it. My younger daughter edited my emotional draft and with her own emotions under control delivered it eloquently.

Some weeks later I carried Peter's ashes to Sydney and, with my old school buddy John as moral support, scattered them over the sea in Manly.

I was the only beneficiary of Peter's modest Will and burst into tears in solicitor Theana Thompson's office in Carnegie when we discussed the details. Through my veil of tears I sobbed, 'I don't want his money... I just want Peter back!'

In these circumstances how many solicitors would pray for their client? But that's what Theana did.

I wondered how Peter would want me to use his money, so I decided if he'd had to make that decision he'd want to help those less fortunate than he'd been. Accordingly I donated funds on his behalf to the 'Come to Lunch' community outreach at St Paul's in North Caulfield as this mission to marginalised and disenfranchised souls was appropriate. Then I donated funds to the Oakleigh Bowling Club with the hope that young men would be encouraged to play this recreational sport. In addition I gave small sums to random charities and prepaid my own funeral so that my family wouldn't have to face that financial burden when the time comes. The small balance has been set aside to help in situations that may face me and my family in the days and hopefully years to come.

CHAPTER 33

DAD NEEDS HELP

A man may perform astonishing feats and comprehend a vast amount of knowledge, and yet have no understanding of himself. But suffering directs a man to look within. If it succeeds, then there, within him, is the beginning of his learning.

Soren Kierkegaard, philosopher

Is it any wonder I was so traumatised by Peter's sudden death? It wasn't just his death, it was the aftermath – the eulogy, the funeral, the scattering of the ashes. Added to this was the fact that I was in the middle of writing a book, sourcing a publisher, arranging publicity for the book launches in Melbourne and Sydney, and in the background knowing that my former wife's condition was continuing to deteriorate. All of this added up to a toxic cocktail and when reality struck I became severely depressed. My children expressed their concern about my mental health and so did my best buddy John in Sydney whom I used as a sounding board. He suggested I take antidepressants, and my daughters encouraged me to get professional help. Being self-reliant I expected the depression to lift. *Wrong!* The clouds were getting darker and I knew it. Self-medication appeared to be the way out, so I sabotaged myself by saying and agreeing with myself, 'I'll have a few beers and things are sure to improve.'[1] *Wrong again!* Things got worse and my world became darker than ever.

It was then I had to face the issue of pride. 'I'm a man… I can beat this… I've done it before and I'll do it again.' Did you know that God has a way of humbling us? He can, and will, bring us to our knees.

One Sunday morning after I'd reassured myself I was going to be OK (just when pride was having its way), I was at St Paul's and pricked up my ears during the preaching when I heard, 'God uses doctors. We have seen many miracles of healing in this church over the years and God is the Chief Physician, but we must never forget the vital role of the medical profession.'

These words rang true for me that morning. It was now time to seek prayer, so I went forward and two strong men of God asked what I needed prayer for.

'I've been severely depressed lately and I can't fathom why.'

Then the leader of the Healing Team at St Paul's enquired, 'Paul, has there been a trigger?'

To which I began to say, 'My… br…o…th…e…r…'

Then crash! I fell to the floor* and lay there like a sack of potatoes. Neither of the men could prevent me from falling. God has His ways of meeting us just at the point of our deepest need!

The following morning I made an appointment with my local general practitioner, and after discussing with her my ongoing depression we agreed to activate a Medical Health Plan (MHP).

First I was visited in my home by an occupational therapist, a gorgeous, athletic young woman (isn't God so thoughtful?), who quickly discerned that the source of my depression was my brother's untimely death. She followed this up by saying, 'If you wish, you can have a psychiatrist visit you or you could see a clinical psychologist.'

In the first instance I elected to meet their psychiatrist, who duly arrived in the pleasing form of another young and very attractive young lady, a final-year medical student. If anyone could have persuaded me to take a course of antidepressants she could, but I knew that medication was not the answer; instead, I opted for five free sessions with a clinical psychologist. As you've noticed by now, I'm good at talking, and talking therapy was just what I needed more than anything else.

I've got you laughing, haven't I? If you've kept up with this story so far, you're sure to agree that it's been one of pain and pathos. At the end of the day, laughter is the best medicine and that's for sure.[2]

1 My legal drug of choice was James Boag's Premium stubbies – 'from the pure waters of Tasmania'.
2 'A cheerful heart is good medicine, but a crushed spirit dries up the bones' (Proverbs 17:22).

PART TWO

Forms of Treatment for Schizophrenia

INTRODUCTION

I suspect a handful of people won't want to read Part One of this book as it digs too close to the bone for those whose lives have been affected by this scourge called schizophrenia. So I'm now cutting to the chase and in this section I'll get to the pointy end of this melodrama, i.e. how to be healed.

Bear with me as I recapitulate events in my life that led to my healing from sexual abuse and be prepared to be shocked. What follows is confronting and may bring back to life memories of your past, events so traumatic that you've hidden them from yourself and from the wider world.

A female nurse sexually abused me as she was changing my nappy when I was six months old.

When I was about twelve I was interfered with by an intellectually handicapped male teenager. At age eighteen I was anally raped by a male stranger. At the time, I thought *that's life* and moved on. I married, fathered children and led a normal life. But the consequences came back to haunt me.

In the early 1970s, due to stress and my frenetic lifestyle as a business executive and overseer of my brother's journey, I lost total interest in having sex. These were the days before Viagra® and I just couldn't get it up and had no desire to do so. We wanted another child so I saw my local doctor who sent me to a sexual therapist.[1] When he took me back to age twelve I began to cry and the box of tissues soon appeared. The remedy for this lack of interest in sex turned out to be extremely practical – no psychotherapy, no drugs, just occupational therapy: 'Have a few days off work and wear less restrictive underpants.'

This therapy worked and it wasn't long before my wife and I conceived another gorgeous daughter, but the psychiatrist hadn't delved deep enough to uncover the root of my problem: sexual abuse.

Fast forward five years and I'm confronted with more extremely stressful situations both at home and at work. Uncharacteristically I found myself having a 'one-off' inappropriate encounter. This awakened something deep within me which at the time I couldn't understand. The past had come up to bite me on the bum. What happened then was to change the course of my married life.

In 1988, after I'd had my born-again experience, the course of my life improved dramatically. Things didn't change immediately (the process is called sanctification*) but I was eventually to conform to the image of the man God had created originally. Christian healing took many years as the extent of the abuse I'd suffered from such an early age was profound and had altered my self-perception. There was much prayer for healing, which included a significant amount of deliverance ministry over many years, here in Australia and in England and Scotland through Ellel Ministries.[2]

The final healing took place some years ago in my lounge room! It was in the depths of winter and I was laid low with pneumonia. Michelle, a friend from St Paul's with whom I'd shared my journey, lent me some books and videos[3] that were to totally set me free from the past. I was finally to be healed from the effects of years of sexual abuse, through Christian healing and deliverance ministry.

Allow me to put a caveat on this conversation before we go further. I have many friends and acquaintances inside and outside the Church who've been sexually abused but can't remember the abuse or have erased it from their subconscious mind. These dear souls know something isn't right but they're stuck. Only those who now seek professional help have the best chance of recovery.

Let me give you a current example. I met an overweight woman at a Christian gathering last week and as we got talking I felt able to share that I'd been sexually abused as a child. She confided in me that she too had been molested in infancy. She eventually married, twice, had a child and left both husbands because they'd abused her. She produced photographs from her handbag of herself as a young, slim and vivacious bride and confided, 'I've made a conscious effort to get fat so that men won't look at me.'

---

1 Who turned out to be a psychiatrist.
2 Here I pay tribute to the wonderful people at Ellel Ministries International: https://peterhorrobin.com/ellel-ministries/
3 Leanne Payne Ministries, especially the book titled *The Broken Image*. Also Elijah House Ministries – Australia.

CHAPTER 1

CONSULTANT PSYCHIATRISTS

THE ROLE OF THE PSYCHIATRIST

Psychiatrists are medical doctors who specialise in diagnosing and treating people with mental illnesses. To become a psychiatrist in Australia and New Zealand a doctor must train for at least six years.

Psychiatrists played a significant role in Peter's life. You will recall it was a highly respected Sydney psychiatrist, Dr William Arnott, who diagnosed his first nervous breakdown and recommended that he should get away from life in Sydney to take on a less stressful job in the country. Peter next encountered psychiatrists in Toowoomba many years later. After that there was an entourage in Queensland and then here in Victoria. From the first diagnosis to the last, treatment included a plethora of alternatives – drugs, electroconvulsive therapy and, finally, the drug of last resort.

I accompanied Peter on some of his visits to psychiatrists and spent many hours pleading with them and with general practitioners in Toowoomba and in Melbourne to help him. It was a psychiatrist who informed me of Peter's attempt at suicide by jumping off the balcony at the Kingston Centre in Melbourne.

My own personal experiences with psychiatrists have been many and varied. Over forty years ago a locum general practitioner diagnosed me as being hypomanic (a mild form of mania, marked by elation and hyperactivity). Of course at the time, this diagnosis was absolutely correct as I wasn't coping with the enormous pressure I was under at home, work and at play. After this diagnosis I made an appointment with a psychiatrist at the Box Hill Hospital who prescribed lithium, which I took for about a week and discontinued after I read about the side effects in the Pharmacopeia.[1]

The next experience with a psychiatrist was in the late 1980s. I was asked to break the law when I was working as a storeman with an Australian multinational company in Mulgrave. I refused to do so, which resulted in huge pressure being placed on me by the management. My psychiatrist, Dr Bill Pring, suggested I could take a short break in the public psychiatric unit at Prince Henry's[2] in St Kilda Road, which seemed a good idea at the time. It now makes me laugh as I tell you this story but it certainly didn't at the time.

Not all good ideas are God's ideas. Consequently I prayed about whether I should go to a 'loony bin' and was given the distinct impression that I was to spend time in this psychiatric unit as a voluntary patient: '*The experience you will gain there, Paul, will be of great value in your future ministry.*'

It was a twelve-bed unit in this run-down concrete jungle called a psychiatric ward and it was very difficult to distinguish the staff from the patients because *they* were so stressed,[3] so with tongue in cheek I asked one of the nurses, 'How do you tell the staff from the patients in here?'

Taking me seriously she replied, 'The staff wear name tags.'

Because this was a teaching hospital I had to tell the students over and over again why I was there. The very attractive young female doctor in her final year before graduating as a psychiatrist decided to interrogate me as I sat in a chair opposite her. She sat on a raised seat with her legs apart so I could see right up her skirt. (She knew exactly what she was doing!) Naturally I averted my gaze and thoughts. Added to that, it was obvious she was flirting with one of the other graduating doctors as she smiled seductively at him each time he walked through the ward.

Each morning at St Henry's the nursing staff began shoving drugs into me as though they were going out of fashion. This concerned me so much that I spat them out at the first opportunity, but this was noticed by the staff, so when the consultant psychiatrist (whom the medical staff worshipped as if he was a god) did his rounds he said, 'If you don't take the drugs, I have the authority to send you to Larundel [a major Melbourne psychiatric hospital].'

The minister from the Uniting Church I was attending, Reverend Dr Roger Bassam, was in the waiting room, so I said to the high and mighty psychiatrist, 'I'll make a decision after I discuss this with my minister.'

The consultant psychiatrist left and Roger came in and we discussed our options.

'Paul, I believe it would be best for you to "play the game" as I'm sure God will be able to use this experience.'

Roger left, I told the boss-cocky I'd take the medication, and he left feeling very satisfied indeed, power struggle over.

The next day, I walked out of Prince Henry's and returned home, not before borrowing the video *One Flew Over the Cuckoo's Nest* from the Mount Waverley video store which I watched as I sat up in bed.

As I was watching the video and realising how real and close to the bone this story was, the phone rang in the kitchen. My wife answered and a muffled discussion followed. I muted the video when she came up to the bedroom to tell me, 'It was the consultant psychiatrist from Prince Henry's. He's very worried about you. He told me that I have the right to commit you to Larundel. They want to give you electroconvulsive therapy [ECT]. I told him I wouldn't give him authority as I know how much you dread shock treatment.'

I spent the afternoon in bed and in the evening watched television with the family and returned to work the next day.

There were to be more encounters with shrinks, not all of them as traumatic as the one I've just recounted.

After our divorce I tried really hard to get the marriage back together. Thinking that meeting with a female psychiatrist was the answer, I contacted Dr Julie Jones, a highly regarded consultant psychiatrist in private practice in South Yarra. Her reputation was impeccable and being a lecturer to students of psychiatry at the University of Melbourne was certainly a recommendation. We could see Dr Jones together but no, Beverley wanted to see the psychiatrist separately.

It was after the one appointment that Beverley made with Dr Jones that I was told at my appointment later that she had no desire to remarry me. So what could I do? I finally had to accept the fact that the marriage was well and truly over.

I was very impressed with the professionalism of Dr Jones. She conscientiously took personal history details in longhand and concluded that I was zealous about my Christian faith (which of course I was). I gained the impression she thought I wanted to 'convert' her, but that was never my aim as conversion is always the work of the Holy Spirit.

Moving on, I found the relocation from Warburton to Melbourne quite stressful – and wouldn't you! Having absolutely no help from family and assistance from only one older friend, I had to navigate downsizing from a three-bedroom home to a one-bedroom home unit. I underestimated the volume of furniture to be taken by the removers and ended up having to do seven runs backwards and forwards with household items stuffed into my small car.

'We're worried about you,' said one daughter to the other after the move, 'we think you should see a psychiatrist.'

To keep peace within the family I reluctantly agreed and made an appointment to see my old friend and fellow Bible College student, consultant psychiatrist Dr John Ouw, at his home office in Ringwood. John opened with, 'Your daughters are very concerned about you, Paul.'

My reply was unequivocal: 'I'm stressed, John. Moving house is no Sunday School picnic …'

John listened, got a bit bored and finally said, 'How's the tennis going? I remember fondly how much Lily and I enjoyed that day we had with you and your wife at your home in Mount Waverley. We enjoyed so much playing tennis on your court.'

I can't recall exactly why or when, but I did seek professional help from a consultant psychiatrist on another occasion. It was possibly during the period I was dealing with the outfall from the Warburton Tennis Club debacle that I found myself on the couch in the Punt Street, South Yarra rooms of a young Jewish psychiatrist. This turned out to be a waste of time and money as the poor young fellow had recently separated from his wife and was dealing with all the pressures associated with that and his two young and confused children. In hindsight I should have rendered him an account or alternatively I could have asked for my consultation fees back, but it didn't really matter.

About two years after moving back to Melbourne I was led by the Holy Spirit to go to Western Australia for a short-term mission and ended up spending a year in a remote mining town 1,000 kilometres north of Perth in a place called Wiluna. Here I was appointed to the teaching staff of a combined kindergarten, primary and secondary school which mainly catered for Aboriginal children. The constant heat, flies, dysfunction and oppression there was extremely difficult to cope with. I returned home quite depressed and, again influenced by my children, sought help from the consultant psychiatrist Dr Neil Hucker in Box Hill, and after three talking therapy sessions I was declared as right as rain.

So there you have it. I've had some good and not-so-good experiences with bats in the belfry and psychiatrists.

1 A book published annually under the jurisdiction of the Government, containing a list of drugs, their formulas, methods of making, side effects, etc.
2 My wife was a Life Governor at St Henry's – a title awarded to her for her voluntary work at the hospital.
3 I poked my head into the staffroom. Most of the staff were smoking furtively. The atmosphere was similar to the caravan park in Doon Reserve.

CHAPTER 2

CLINICAL PSYCHOLOGISTS

THE ROLE OF THE PSYCHOLOGIST

A psychologist is a professional who evaluates and studies behaviour and mental processes. Psychologists must have completed a university degree in psychology which is a master's degree in some countries and a doctorate in others. This definition of psychologist is non-exclusive; in most jurisdictions, members of other professions (such as counsellors and psychiatrists) can also evaluate, diagnose, treat and study mental processes. Some psychologists, such as clinical and counselling psychologists, provide mental health care and some psychologists, such as social or organisational psychologists, conduct research and provide consultation services.[1]

THE DIFFERENCE BETWEEN
A PSYCHIATRIST AND A PSYCHOLOGIST

Although psychologists and psychiatrists can be said to share a same fundamental aim – the alleviation of mental distress – their training, outlook and methodologies are often quite different. Perhaps the most significant difference is that psychiatrists are licensed physicians. As such, psychiatrists often use the medical model to assess mental health problems and rely on psychotropic medications as the chief method of addressing mental health problems. Clinical psychologists receive extensive training in psychological test administration, scoring, interpretation and reporting.

A patient with a complicated clinical presentation who is being seen by a psychiatrist might be referred to a clinical psychologist for psychological testing to aid in diagnosis and treatment. In addition, psychologists, particularly those from PhD programmes, spend several years in graduate school being trained to conduct behavioural research, including research design and advanced statistical analysis. While this training is available for physicians it is not typically in medical education. Conversely, psychiatrists as licensed physicians have received training more broadly in other areas such as medicine and neurology and may bring this knowledge to bear in identifying and treating medical or neurological conditions that can present similarly to psychiatric diseases.

Psychologists generally do not prescribe medication although in some (US) jurisdictions psychologists have limited prescribing privileges. Clinical and other psychologists are experts in psychotherapy (typically clinical psychologists are trained in a number of psychological therapies, including behavioural, cognitive, humanistic, existential, psychodynamic and systematic approaches), and psychological testing (e.g. including neuropsychological testing).[2]

As far as Peter was concerned I'm not aware of any appointments with clinical psychologists, although I'm not privy to all of Peter's medical appointments. I do know that the many general practitioners Peter was referred to would have done their utmost to talk with Peter in an endeavour to sort through his mental problems as well as prescribing many and varied drugs over time.

My experience with clinical psychologists was only recent and, as mentioned earlier, happened after the shock and trauma experienced due to Peter's sudden and unanticipated death.

To reiterate, after Peter died I dropped my bundle completely. I was in total disbelief that the brother whose care I'd overseen for more than thirty years was no longer there, so I made an appointment with my general practitioner Dr Leonie Ross at the Chadstone Clinic. In our many consultations, as usual, Dr Ross was most understanding and suggested that I might like to see Dr Hucker, whom she had recommended after the experience in remote Western Australia. But for me I couldn't afford the fees and I didn't want to drive to Box Hill in my present state. Then Dr Ross suggested an alternative solution which would provide an assessment by an occupational therapist in my home, to be followed up by whatever was recommended in that meeting.[3] This idea appealed to me so I agreed to begin the process.

In due course, as written earlier and repeated for emphasis, there was a knock on my door to behold a young and pretty

South African Jewish occupational therapist. After an hour of listening to me it was obvious to her that the reason I was depressed was Peter's sudden death. She suggested that I could have a psychiatrist call to see me or I could continue to meet with her. I chose to check out the psychiatrist option and, lo and behold, a week later a young, good-looking Jewish trainee psychiatrist appeared at my door. (I thought all my Christmases had come at once!) Wide-eyed and bushy-tailed, she was determined to get me to take antidepressants, which to me wasn't kosher. (If anyone could have talked me into anything, this cutie could, but I graciously declined.) Instead, I opted to see a clinical psychologist with a natural preference for a Christian, but by prayer and supplication I knew that the person recommended was the man to see. I immediately made an appointment to see a Dr David Spektor at Psychology Care in Malvern.

Here was a man I could relate to immediately. Unlike most psychiatrists who feel quite affronted when asking them about their personal lives, David at our very first meeting told me about himself and after doing so invited me to ask questions. For me this was truly a breath of fresh air, which gave me the confidence to reveal everything about myself.

In the many meetings that followed, which I always scheduled on Thursday afternoons after I'd participated in the Healing Service at St Paul's which is in walking distance to David's rooms (and my favourite Continental cake shop, Fleischer's in Glenferrie Road), I unravelled my sad story about my journey with Peter. I left no stone unturned as I unearthed my interpretation of the life that took me from our cradles to Peter's grave.

Our meetings were not all a one-way street. I was able to share my Christian faith comfortably with David and quoted many passages, from both the New Testament and the writings of David and the prophets Isaiah and Jeremiah in the Scriptures, some of which were familiar to him. It was not my intention to proselyt-ise David, but only God knows what transactions were taking place in our meetings. David wouldn't be the first Messianic Jew in Melbourne – nor would he be the last.

1 Psychologist – Wikipedia (edited).
2 Contrast with psychiatrist – Wikipedia (edited).
3 A Mental Health Plan (MHP).

CHAPTER 3

CHRISTIAN HEALING AND DELIVERANCE

For our struggle is not against flesh and blood, but against the rulers, against the authorities, against the powers of this dark world and against the spiritual forces of evil in the heavenly realms.

Ephesians 6:12

For though we live in the world, we do not wage war as the world does. The weapons we fight with are not the weapons of the world. On the contrary, they have divine power to demolish strongholds. We demolish arguments and every pretension that sets itself up against the knowledge of God, and we take captive every thought to make it obedient to Christ.

2 Corinthians 10:3–5

M ost Christians and certainly unbelievers don't know they're in a battle. We're in a war, a spiritual war, and most of us have no protection against the forces of evil.

The Church hasn't dealt with the powers of darkness as an enlightened and united body. Here and there, individuals have been raised up by God to make significant inroads into the vast territory over which the devil holds such undisputed sway. Fortunately God has restored to the Church a good measure of the Pentecostal power and authority so vividly demonstrated in the early Church. Numbers of believers have received the baptism of the Holy Spirit* and the gifts of the Spirit, and as they entered into conflict with the powers of darkness they began to discover the presence and activity of evil spirits, not only in unbelievers, but to their surprise and shock, also in Christians. The spiritual, that is, the mature Christian understands that it is Satan and his wicked spirits who move powerfully behind the events of our time.

What happens to someone who's born again? Do the Scriptures teach that the new birth includes *automatic expulsion* of demons? No. All human beings are under the influence of the evil one,[1] and his influence over mankind is exercised by evil spirits. But in the new birth, the infant believer has his (or her) sins forgiven. His spirit – formerly dead in trespasses and sins – is made alive by the Spirit of God and a person receives power to become a son (or daughter) of God. He now begins to have the power to overcome the very things which enslaved him before. What a marvellous change from victim of sin to victory over sin – joint victor with Christ.[2]

Nowhere do the Scriptures or experience teach that the new birth automatically eliminates demon influence or bondage, or for that matter, all of the remnants of the old nature such as tempers, moods, lusts, envying, selfishness, prejudice, to name a few. The born-again believer must learn to take up his cross, deny himself and die daily; he must walk in the Spirit to prevent the lust of his flesh having its way. Hopefully he will also press on to find his rightful place in the plan of God and effectual functioning in the Body of Christ*. The process of growing up in Christ is usually painful, though the result is glorious. The most painful part is the discovery of certain areas in which the believer has been deceived. Oh how we need prayer for healing and deliverance in the Australian Church and the Church universal today!

As I reflect on what I've written above, I'm reminded of that wonderful day some years back when Peter was born again. We both attended Sunday School at St Matthew's in Manly where we were Christened and confirmed, but neither of us had the new birth experience. It wasn't until I took Peter to my mate Carlton's home that Carlton and I led Peter in the sinner's prayer, followed by a prayer of repentance. Peter was now gloriously saved. Unfortunately at this time he wasn't healed or delivered from the demonic forces that so crippled him. It took years for me to stand in the gap for Peter and eventually see him conformed to the image of Christ.

Time is a great readjuster of perspective, so after my wonderful John Wesley experience[3] on 24 May 1988 and my close-to-death experience in the Upper Yarra Valley later, I thought I was home and hosed. I'm born again, I've received the baptism with the Holy Spirit – I'm set free. Hallelujah. But how deceived can you be! I knew nothing about deliverance; consequently I found myself continuing to do things outside the will of God. I was ignorant of blessings and curses made so clear in chapter 28 in the book of Deuteronomy in the Old Testament. I discovered that as a result of my father's and his father's involvement in Freemasonry, the Penman family line was under a curse. A curse was also operating in the matriarchal line, the McCombie clan, but thanks be to God, both curses have now been broken through persevering in prayer.

As a consequence of these curses having been broken, I'm living the glorious life God promised.

1 'As for you, you were dead in your transgressions and sins, in which you used to live when you followed the ways of this world and of the ruler of the kingdom of the air, the spirit that is now at work in those who are disobedient. All of us also lived among them at one time, gratifying the cravings of our sinful nature and following its desires and thoughts. Like the rest, we were by nature objects of wrath' (Ephesians 2:1–3).
2 This is a heavily edited version of the Foreword in Jessie Penn-Lewis's book. See Bibliography for details.
3 John Wesley, founder of Methodism, had a remarkable Holy Spirit experience in Aldersgate Street, London, on 24 May 1738. (See John Wesley diaries in the Bibliography.) Of interest, Hillary Clinton was raised in the Methodist tradition.

WE'VE COME A LONG
WAY, BABY

How one does end a book like this? I'll leave you with two quotes.

The first is from a book I've been reading, *Unparalleled Sorrow* by Barry Dickins. Here's what Barry has to say:

> This was our family's downfall, the obsession with there being something wrong. It's called Munchausen's syndrome.[1] The only thing wrong with my mother was boredom, so she made sure she got her fix (she took heaps of prescribed drugs – Serapax, Valium, Bex, et al) and she grew worse and stayed that way forever. She would have been a lot better off playing tennis or running a hot bath or reading. We stopped having people over and she grew worse and stayed that way forever.[2]

The second reading comes from the man often referred to as the 'father of modern psychotherapy', Carl Jung (1875–1961):

Anyone who wants to know the human psyche will learn next to nothing from experimental psychology. He would be better advised to abandon exact science, put away his scholar's gown, bid farewell to his study, *and wander with human heart throughout the world* [my italics]. There in the horrors of prisons, lunatic asylums and hospitals, in drab suburban pubs, in brothels and gambling-hells, in the salons of the elegant, the Stock Exchanges, Socialist meetings, churches, revivalist gatherings and ecstatic sects, through love and hate, through the experience of passion in every form in his own body, he would reap richer stores of knowledge than text-books a foot thick would give him, and he will know how to doctor the sick with a real knowledge of the human soul.[3]

How many of us who recite the Lord's Prayer understand what it means when we say the words 'deliver us from evil'? Some translations of the Bible read 'deliver us from the evil one'.

We ALL need deliverance from the powers of darkness!

I recall clearly the word of my father when I was a young man applying for jobs. He would say, 'Don't mention anything about mental illness in the family.'

At the time, I used to say to myself, *What's Dad talking about? What's mental illness?*

There was such a stigma about mental illness in those days, and nothing much has changed in spite of the hard work by organisations such as Beyondblue and Bravehearts and the sustained work of people like Rosie Batty, Ita Buttrose, Jeff Kennett, Patrick McGorry et al. In spite of what the media wants to tell us, just to mention mental illness in polite Australian circles is definitely a no-go zone. But things are slowly changing and I thank God for that.

If only my grandmother back in central western New South Wales had been given the right treatment for her damaged uterus, and healing and deliverance ministry for post-traumatic stress and other curses, would she have ended up in a lunatic asylum? The book by Jessie Penn-Lewis had not then been written and Carl Jung was in vogue. Who knew anything about healing and deliverance and the reality of the demonic realm? The Lord's Prayer for most was a recitation.

In 1912, when *War on the Saints* was first published, how many people thought Penn-Lewis was mad? A quick read of the early pages of the book shows how much spiritual warfare was being conducted against her and her co-author, Welsh Revivalist Evan Roberts.

If only my dear mother's doctors knew then what they know today, would she have spent most of her married life in and out of nursing homes, surviving electroconvulsive therapy, bathroom cupboards full of prescribed drugs, boxes of tissues and endless hours on the psychiatrists' couches?

And what about Peter, my big brother, trying to fight the battle against the scourge of schizophrenia? Without the Holy Spirit and the gift of the word of knowledge, who would have ever known that he had been sexually abused, the revelation of which was to be the root cause of this diagnosis?[4]

It's vital to know at the outset what's at the root of the problem besetting the presenting patient; otherwise the medical profession is playing Russian roulette. This book is therefore a challenge to the medical profession and to mature Christians to wake up! It's time to end the roller-coaster ride on unnecessary and over-prescribed drugs, overuse of electroconvulsive therapy, and excessive appointments with clinical psychologists and consultant psychiatrists. These words will fly in the face of conventional wisdom, but true Wisdom comes from above. It's time for an open discussion.

I thank God I've been healed and delivered! It certainly didn't happen overnight; it took years. Today I can truly say I'm living the abundant life that God promises to all who believe and trust in his Son, our Saviour, Jesus Christ. The Lord is my joy, my strength and my salvation. Hallelujah.

I once heard someone say, 'Why don't they do something?'
Why don't *you* do something?

Heaven's real!
When I get there I hope to hear my mother say, 'Thanks, Paul.'
I hope to hear Peter say, 'Good on yer, little brother.'
I hope to hear the Lord say, 'Well done, good and faithful servant.'

1 A condition in which a person intentionally fakes, simulates, worsens or self-induces an illness (including psychiatric) for the main purpose of drawing attention to themselves and therefore being treated like a medical patient.
2 Barry Dickins, *Unparalleled Sorrow: Finding My Way Back from Depression*, Hardie Grant Books (2010), p. 37.
3 C. G. Jung, *The Collected Works, Volumes I–XX*, ed. Herbert Read, Routledge (2015), pp. 2890–1.
4 During the prayer ministry for Peter at St Paul's, the Holy Spirit revealed that there was a curse over the Penman family line as a consequence of their generational involvement with Freemasonry. There was also a curse over the McCombie family line due to their generational involvement with the occult.

POSTSCRIPT

Saint Peter

He won't try to get a chorus
Out of lungs that's worn to rags,
Or to graft the wings on shoulders
That is stiff with humpin' swags.
But I'll rest about the station
Where the work-bell never rings,
Till they blow the final trumpet
And the Great Judge sees to things.

Henry Lawson, 'Verses Popular and Humorous'
A Camp-Fire Yarn: Complete Works 1885–1900, verse 6
(p 275)

SCHIZOPHRENIA AND DEMON POSSESSION

[AUTHOR'S COMMENT: This is the opinion of Pastor Deoki but many Christian leaders would challenge that ALL are demon possessed.]

Sydney's Callan Park Hospital for the Insane (1878–1914) was the first purpose-built hospital for 'moral therapy' treatment in Australia. Notable inmates were the poet Henry Lawson's mother, suffragette Louisa Lawson and her sons Charles and Peter. Notable too was J. F. Archibald, editor and publisher of *The Bulletin*.[1] On this site today stands the Sydney College of the Arts (SCA), the visual arts faculty of the University of Sydney.

I was talking recently with my mate and pastor, Carlton Deoki,[2] and we were reminiscing about our earlier working days in Sydney. Carlton quipped, 'Soon after I arrived in Australia from Fiji, I spent some time in Callan Park Mental Hospital.'

With a grin on his face he added, 'Gotcha. I worked there for two years training to be a psychiatric nurse!'

Carlton was aware that I'd commenced research for this book so I asked him to give me some impressions of his time working in a lunatic asylum.

'It was in 1963. I was nineteen and even though my dear grandmother, a staunch Methodist, prayed for me, I wasn't yet a Christian. What I saw in Callan Park was people in catatonic states, others walking around muttering to themselves and salivating. I used to have to dispense the drug Largactil. Many were retired soldiers from World War Two, traumatised due to battle shock. I had a heart of compassion for each one of them, but those poor souls were out of their minds.'

At that point Carlton stopped talking. He was visibly moved as he recalled those days long gone.

'Some years after becoming a Christian in 1992, I spent hours immersed in reading God's Word – the Bible. I read other books too, by internationally recognised men of God such as Derek Prince [see www.derekprince.com] and Bill Subritsky [www.dove-ministries.com]. I became involved with the Australian ministry Oz Challenge [www.ozchallenge.org.au], and after attending many of their seminars I became part of their ministry team. When I reflected on my experiences with those dear souls in Callan Park years ago, I became convinced that they were all demon possessed.'[3]

My ears pricked up when Carlton said they were 'all demon possessed', so I asked, 'Could *all* of these people be demon possessed?'

'Yes. Grief and trauma leave the door wide open for Satan to take a stronghold in their lives and it is only the ministry of the Holy Spirit that can set them free. This is spiritual warfare.'

I recalled that Carlton had recently been a guest speaker at a weekend camp organised by his church in Melton where he was invited to speak on the subject of Spiritual Warfare. Carlton invited me to attend as his prayer partner, as we have both had to do battle with the forces of evil many times over.

After Carlton's sound foundational teaching to a large audience of mainly new Christians, we prayed for some who came forward, but it was obvious to both of us that the majority of the people in the audience were not convinced that there was such a thing as a spirit realm or spiritual warfare.

'Carlton, what happened as a result of your teaching?'

'A week or so after the camp the pastor was searching the internet and came across a teaching that debunked spiritual warfare, so he shared his findings with his congregation and as a result the church is still in spiritual deception where I had found it when I joined earlier in the year.' Carlton added, 'I don't attend that church any more. You know, Paul, the internet is the devil's playground.'

---

1 *The Bulletin* ceased publication in 2008 after 128 years. J. F. Archibald was the founder of the New South Wales Art Gallery's Archibald Prize. The 2016 prize was won by Louise Hearman for her portrait of Oz icon Barry Humphries.

2 Carlton is a son of Andrew Inder Narayan Deoki OBE (dec.), a Christian in the Methodist tradition and a former Attorney General of Fiji (1979–1981).

3 Recommended reading for church leaders: *War on the Saints*. See Bibliography. Request the Oz Challenge manual, *Personal & Strategic Level Spiritual Warfare*.

A LETTER TO ONE OF AUSTRALIA'S LEADING PSYCHIATRISTS

Saturday 21 November 2015

Professor David J. Castle
Chair of Psychiatry, St Vincent's Hospital
The University of Melbourne

Dear David

Re: Treatment Strategies in Schizophrenia

I am so grateful that you could spare some of your valuable time to see me yesterday to discuss the book I'm currently researching – *A Life Unfulfilled: The Scourge of Schizophrenia.*[1]

As promised, I've enclosed a signed copy of my latest book *Why Did Grandpa Go to Africa?* and thank you for the two books you so generously gave me. I do hope and pray that you will have time to read about my exciting adventures in your beloved South Africa and countries beyond.

Also enclosed is a barrage of paperwork. (Please forgive me.) Some of this I read to you yesterday. There are two 'light' pieces which are examples of my current writing. *Enjoy.*

Of particular significance in the paperwork enclosed are the Google references to 'Born Again' and the 'Word of Knowledge'. You're sure to find this absorbing reading.

I'm confident we can collaborate on my book if you are agreeable to do so. I'll need to run some draft pages past you, especially when I write about the role of psychiatrists in the healing process for schizophrenia. And naturally, I'll give you the appropriate credits when the book is eventually published. As discussed, I have no time frame to get the book out. It will take as long as it takes. Perhaps Melbourne University Press or Oxford University Press will take a punt on it?!!!

I used the word 'testable' a number of times in our meeting. I have living and breathing evidence that God heals, and heals today – not just schizophrenia, but cancer, etc., etc. You have all of the Research Modelling facilities at your disposal to prove conclusively that what I've witnessed is true.

I believe the research results undertaken by the University of Melbourne[2] will be groundbreaking.

Time is *not* of the essence with this research project which may be tailored to a PhD student. Absolute integrity in the methodology of the research is paramount. I know you'll agree.

I'll look forward to another chat when you have the time available.

May God bless you abundantly, David.

(Signed) Paul Penman
FAIA TPAA BA BSSC (Hons) GradDipArts (Writing)

I have no doubt that Professor Castle is an extremely busy man. In fact I was surprised that he could make time to see me, but as he wrote in an email, he was particularly interested in the subject of schizophrenia.[3]

---

1 This was a working title of the book which has since been changed to *Victory Over Schizophrenia: My Journey with Peter.*

2 It doesn't have to be the University of Melbourne! Other universities are welcome to be part of a study, so I especially encourage the following Victorian universities to consider this original research opportunity: Australian Catholic University, Deakin University, Federation University, La Trobe University, Monash University, RMIT University, Swinburne University and Victoria University.

3 See Bibliography to reference scholarly books David has written on the subject of schizophrenia.

MY EXPERIENCE OF HEAVEN
(Heaven is real)

'Where will I go when I die?' Sound familiar? On Easter Day, Sunday 26 March 2016, I got a view of heaven and this is what I saw.

WE ARE SEATED WITH CHRIST
IN HEAVENLY PLACES

And God raised us up with Christ and seated us with him in the heavenly realms in Christ Jesus, in order that in the coming ages he might show the incomparable riches of his grace …

Ephesians 2:6–7; see also Isaiah 6

I awoke this morning drunk! I was drunk in the Holy Spirit.

Last night I attended the monthly gathering of Christians at the home of Michael and Elizabeth Szabo in

Endeavour Hills. This fellowship, called God Is Love, has been operating for thirty years. Michael and Elizabeth's younger son is my son-in-law.

Unlike most traditional Christian services or masses, the proceedings lasted for over three hours. The Holy Spirit was invited at the outset and accepted the invitation and remained throughout.

The praise and worship segment was led by my daughter and her husband. This was followed by what is called an 'activation', which was led by guest preachers Pam and her husband Andrew. We were invited by Pam to enter into heaven spiritually, and here is what I saw.

The cross of Christ was laid down as a bridge to walk from this realm into the heavens, where I saw Jesus walking around in prayer. In front of me to my left was my mother, looking at me. My brother Peter was holding her hand. They were both totally relaxed and at eternal peace. As I approached them they smiled at me as if to say, 'We're home at last.' I couldn't see my father. At the time, this is all I saw.

This morning after a really deep sleep I asked the Lord to show me more. I was immediately given a picture of the male mentors whom God had positioned on my path along my life's troubled journey. First there was my Sunday School teacher Ron Watkins, then my first minister, the Reverend A. R. Ebbs; then there appeared a man whose name I've forgotten, a strong male role-model in my early years when I worked in advertising. Then there was a minister at the Uniting Church in Mount Waverley, and strikingly, during the breakdown of our marriage, there was the Reverend Emeritus Professor George Yuille who at this disastrous time had written me the most encouraging letter. The Lord showed me these people, assuring me that

141

through them He had never left me nor had He forsaken me, especially at these tormented times in my life. Hallelujah! Hallelujah! Hallelujah!

Then the Lord said to me, '*Now, I have given you the indwelling Holy Spirit, the counsellor, the eternal mentor.*' We are indeed seated with God in heavenly places and there I want to remain. Praise be to God!

P.S. Have a look at what others have to say about heaven at www. heavenvisit.com

THE POWER OF PRAYER

This testimony[1] will be closer to home for most of you. You've read how my brother was healed from schizophrenia through prayer; now read about how the power of prayer changed the course of a substantial Melbourne business.

I have two dear friends in their seventies who've been happily married for over fifty years. Let's call them Darby and Joan, not their real names of course. Due to an unforeseen financial crisis they decided to get out of debt by working part-time in a well-known hardware store not far from their home in Melbourne. As it happened this branch of the multinational conglomerate was the most profitable in Victoria. Their role was as 'people greeters', that is, they welcomed people as they entered the store and bade them farewell as they left.

Darby and Joan were prayerful Christians and naturally each morning as they drove to work would pray the Lord's Prayer into the store. In addition, as each person entered the store they would welcome them with a smile and underneath their breath would pray for them, and as they left they'd do the same thing. Because they lived in the neighbourhood they were able to offer help such as delivering goods for people who couldn't afford the delivery charges, and also direct customers to other stores if their store didn't stock what the customer wanted.

Over a period of seven years, when Darby and Joan's financial crisis had been overcome, they reluctantly decided to retire, much to the disappointment of the staff and management. It wasn't long before the turnover began to decrease and petty theft was on the increase.

Darby and Joan prayed according to God's will. Their prayer was simple but effective and this is what they prayed: 'I speak the name of Jesus into the heart and mind and soul of the person entering the store. I bless them with every good thing and the knowledge of Jesus as they leave the store. I put the store's stamp on the children's hands, telling them that they are special.'

Then silently they prayed, 'Because God made you special He never makes mistakes.'

1 Transcribed verbatim from Joan's recent email.

GLOSSARY

Anointing: The special gifting of the presence of God, enabling one to act with supernatural ease – even in the most difficult of circumstances.

Balm of Gilead: A fragrant medicinal resin obtained from certain trees which represents the soothing healing power of God.

Baptism of the Holy Spirit: The work of God whereby the Holy Spirit places the believer into union with Christ and into union with others. See Acts 1:4–5 and 11:16.

Body of Christ: All those who call themselves Christians.

Born-again Christian: The phenomenon whereby one is transformed into a closer, intimate relationship with Jesus Christ. See John 3:3–5.

Charismatic: Christians who share with Pentecostals an emphasis on the gifts of the Holy Spirit but who remain part of the mainline church.

Deliverance/deliverance ministry: The activity of cleansing a person or property of demonic infestation through prayer and fasting.

Demonic realm: The supernatural realm where evil spirits dwell/reside.

Demonised: To be taken captive by evil spirits.

Electroconvulsive therapy (ECT): A procedure done under general anaesthesia in which small electric currents are passed through the brain, intentionally triggering a brief seizure. ECT, formerly known as 'shock treatment', seems to cause changes in brain chemistry that can quickly reverse symptoms of certain mental illnesses.

Fast: Doing without food and/or drink in order to seek a closer encounter with God and also for success in healing and deliverance prayer. See Matthew 6:16.

Fell to the floor: A form of involuntary prostration in which an individual falls to the floor and may sometimes experience religious ecstasy.

Forces of evil: Those spirits and people who do not give homage to God. See Ephesians 6:12.

Frontal lobe dementia: The name given to dementia when it is due to progressive damage to the frontal and/or temporal lobes of the brain.

Healing Service: A Christian gathering where the congregation pray and/or lay hands on the afflicted to elicit divine intervention to bring about physical and spiritual healing.

Healing Team: Three or more people praying for God's anointing, healing and deliverance.

Holy Spirit: The third person of the Holy Trinity. He is fully God – eternal, omniscient and omnipresent. He is alive, has a will and can speak.

Intercede/intercessory prayer: Group of believers who invoke God's mercy through prayer and fasting on behalf of themselves or others for healing and deliverance.

Lord: Jesus Christ is named the Lord of Lords and King of Kings in the New Testament, and we are told that every knee shall bow and every tongue confess that Jesus Christ is Lord!

Manifested: Display a quality or feeling by one's acts or appearance. The revelation of God's plan in the Bible is a manifestation of God's power and authority in the act of Creation. See Mark 4:22; John 17:6; Romans 3:21; Timothy 3:16.

Martyr complex: Someone who sees himself or herself as a perpetual victim of others.

Passion of Christ: The short and final period in the life of Jesus, covering his entrance to Jerusalem, his betrayal, his arrest and trial, leading to his crucifixion and death on Mount Calvary.

Pentecostal: A renewal movement within Protestant Christianity that places special emphasis on a direct personal experience of God through the baptism of the Holy Spirit.

Primitive Methodist: Primitive Methodism, a religion of popular culture, initiated by John Wesley, was a major movement in English Methodism from about 1810 until the Methodist Union in 1932.

Psychosis: A severe mental disorder that causes abnormal thinking, behaviour and perception.

Ruling spirit: The most senior evil spirit in the hierarchy of evil spirits who controls the torment and possession of the victim.

Sanctification: Continual growth in purity and holiness.

Scriptures: The Holy Scriptures are the sacred writings of the Old and New Testaments.

Spirituality: Christian spirituality is biblically defined as the practice of the Christian faith as derived from the New Testament with the promptings of the Holy Spirit. It includes both knowledge and action. See James 1:25.

Spiritual warfare: 'Our battle is against spiritual powers.' See Ephesians 6:11–16. As Christians we are called to come against all manifestations of the enemy (the devil or evil spirits) in whatever guise they appear, spiritually, mentally and physically.

Stand in the gap: Prayerfully standing in the place of one or more people in the context of intercessory prayer, as Jesus did – He stood in the gap for all of mankind so that we could have the righteousness of God. See also Ezekiel 22:30.

Wait on God: Be still, wait and listen for God's 'still, small voice' – which is best heard during prayer and solitude. See Isaiah 40:31.

Witchcraft: The practice of magic, especially black magic: the use of spells and the invocation of evil spirits. The Bible expressly condemns all forms of witchcraft – including 'white witchcraft'!

Word of God: The phrase 'Word of God' is applied to the Bible in that all sacred Scripture is one means by which God speaks to us. In another sense it applies to Jesus who is the 'Logos of God' – the Word made flesh, i.e. Jesus. See John 1:1.

Word of knowledge: The ability of one person to know what God is currently doing or intends to do in the life of another person. It can also be defined as knowing the secrets of another person's heart. A message of special knowledge by means of the gift of the Holy Spirit. See 1 Corinthians 12:8.

BIBLIOGRAPHY

Bentall, Richard P. *Madness Explained: Psychosis and Human Nature.* Penguin Books, London, UK. 2004.

Bergner, Mario. *Setting Love in Order.* Baker, Grand Rapids, MI, USA. 1993.

Blainey, Geoffrey. *A Short History of Christianity.* Penguin, Camberwell, AUS. 2011.

Bonhoeffer, Dietrich. *The Cost of Discipleship.* SCM Press, London, UK. 1948.

Boyle, Mary. *Schizophrenia: A Scientific Delusion?* (2nd ed.) Routledge, Abingdon, UK. 2002.

Cairns-Smith, A. G., *Evolving the Mind.* Cambridge University Press, Cambridge, UK. 1996.

Castle, David J. and Buckley, Peter F. *Schizophrenia.* Oxford University Press, Oxford, UK. 2015.

Church, Leslie F. *The Early Methodist People.* Epworth Press, London, UK. 1948.

Clark, Randy. *The Biblical Guidebook to Deliverance*. Charisma House, Lake Mary, FL, USA. 2015.

Coles, Robert. *The Mind's Fate*. Little, Brown & Co., New York, USA. 1975.

Collins, Gary R. *Christian Counselling*. Word Publishing, Milton Keynes, UK. 1988.

Crabb, Larry. *Effective Biblical Counselling*. Zondervan, Grand Rapids, MI, USA. 1977.

Cross, Mark and Hanrahan, Catherine. *Changing Minds*. Harper Collins, Sydney, AUS. 2016.

Deveson, Anne. *Tell Me I'm Here*. Penguin Books, Ringwood, AUS. 1998.

Dickins, Barry. *Unparalleled Sorrow*. Hardie Grant Books, Richmond, Victoria, AUS. 2010.

Eavis, Sid. *A Healing Ministry*. Bookbound Publishing, Ourimbah, AUS. 2007.

Ehrenburg, Robert and Sophie. *The Toowoomba Book*. Fidolu, Toowoomba, AUS. 1992.

Erickson, Millard J. *Christian Theology*. Baker Book House, Grand Rapids, MI, USA. 1983.

Foster, David Kyle, *Healing for Sexual Brokenness*. Ellel Ministries, Sydney, AUS. 2005.

Fraser, N., Toovey, A. and Castle, D. *Caring for a Loved One with Psychosis or Schizophrenia*. St Vincent's Hospital, Melbourne, AUS. 2014.

Freed, Sandie. *Breaking the Threefold Demonic Cord*. Chosen Books, Grand Rapids, MI, USA. 2008.

Freud, Sigmund. *The Unconscious*. Penguin Books, London, UK. 1911.

Getz, Gene A. *The Measure of a Man*. Regal Books, Ventura, CA, USA. 1974.

Glennon, Jim. *How Can I Find Healing?* Bridge Publishing, South Plainfield, NJ, USA. 1984.

Gottesman, Irving I. *Schizophrenia Genesis: The Origins of Madness.* Henry Holt & Co., New York, USA. 1990.

Graham, Billy. *Angels: God's Secret Agents.* Doubleday, New York, USA. 1975.

Griffin, Paul and Liz. *Hope and Healing for the Abused.* Sovereign World, Lancaster, UK. 2007.

Hammond, Frank and Ida. *Pigs in the Parlour: A Practical Guide to Deliverance.* RoperPenberthy Publishing, Weybridge, UK. 1973.

Horrobin, David. *The Madness of Adam and Eve: How Schizophrenia Shaped Humanity.* Bantam Press, Ealing, UK. 2001.

Horrobin, Peter. *Healing through Deliverance. Volume 1.* Sovereign World, Kent, UK. 1991.

Horrobin, Peter. *Healing through Deliverance. Volume 2.* Sovereign World, Kent, UK. 1991.

Horrobin, Peter. *Investigating Discernment and Deception.* CD set, Ellel Ministries, AUS. 2006.

Humphrey, Nicholas. *A History of the Mind.* Simon & Schuster, New York, USA. 1992.

Jackel, Graeme. *Blessings for End Times.* Self-Published, Melbourne, AUS. 2000.

Jeffs, Sandy. *Poems from the Madhouse.* Spinifex Press, North Melbourne, AUS. 1993.

Johnson, George. *Fire in the Mind.* Penguin Books, London, UK. 1995.

Laing, R. D. *The Divided Self.* PCCS Books, Ross-on-Wye, UK. 1960.

Leader, Darian. *Strictly Bipolar.* Penguin Books, London, UK. 2013.

Leaf, Carolyn. *Switch On Your Brain.* Baker Book House, Grand Rapids, MI, USA. 2007.

Liardon, Roberts. *God's Generals.* Albury Publishing, Tulsa, OK, USA. 1996.

McMillen, S. I. *None of These Diseases.* Lakeland, London, UK. 1963.

Meyer, Joyce. *The Root of Rejection*. Harrison House, Tulsa, OK, USA. 1994.

Miller, Rachel and Mason, Susan E. *Diagnosis: Schizophrenia*. Columbia University Press, New York, USA. 2002

Nasar, Sylvia. *A Beautiful Mind*. Faber & Faber, London, UK. 1998.

Nichols, Alan. *David Penman*. Albatross Books, Sutherland, AUS. 1991.

Office of Health Economics. *Schizophrenia*. White Crescent Press, Luton, UK. 1979.

Osborne, Grant R. *The Hermeneutical Spiral*. InterVarsity Press, Downers Grove, IL, USA. 1991.

Payne, Leanne. *The Broken Image*. Baker, Grand Rapids, MI, USA. 1995.

Payne, Leanne. *Healing Homosexuality*. Baker, Grand Rapids, MI, USA. 1996.

Peck, M. Scott. *The Road Less Travelled and Beyond*. Simon & Schuster, New York, USA. 1997.

Penn-Lewis, Jessie and Roberts, Evan. *War on the Saints*. Thomas E. Lowe, New York, USA. 1973.

Penman, Paul. *The God of a Second Chance*. Swinburne University, Lilydale, AUS. 2001.

Penman, Paul. *Why Did Grandpa Go to Africa?* Zaccmedia, Preston, UK. 2014.

Prince, Derek. *The Spirit-Filled Believer's Handbook*. Word Publishing, Milton Keynes, UK. 1993.

Prince, Derek. *They Shall Expel Demons*. Chosen Books, Grand Rapids, MI, USA. 1998.

Purnell, Sonia. *First Lady*. Aurum Press, London, UK. 2015.

Ramsland, John. *Brave and Bold*. Brolga Publishing, Melbourne, AUS. 2008.

Saks, Elyn R. *The Centre Cannot Hold: My Journey through Madness*. Hachette Books, New York, USA. 2007.

Sandford, John and Paula. *Restoring the Christian Family.* Victory House Publishers, Tulsa, OK, USA. 1980.

Sandford, Paula. *Healing Victims of Sexual Abuse.* Victory House Publishers, Tulsa, OK, USA, 2009.

Sanford, Agnes. *The Healing Gifts of the Spirit.* Harper Collins, New York, USA, 1984.

Shorter, Edward. *A History of Psychiatry.* John Wiley & Sons, New York, USA. 1997.

Siever, Larry J. and Frucht, William. *The New View of Self.* Macmillan, New York, USA. 1997.

Stone, Michael H. *Healing the Mind: A History of Psychiatry from Antiquity to the Present.* W. W. Norton & Company, New York, USA. 1997.

Subritzky, Bill. *Demons Defeated.* Sovereign World, Chichester, UK. 1985.

Szasz, Thomas. *The Myth of Mental Illness.* Hoeber-Harper, New York, USA. 1961.

Taylor, Harold. *Sent to Heal.* The Order of Luke the Physician, Ringwood, AUS. 1993.

Torrey, E. Fuller. *Surviving Schizophrenia: A Family Manual.* Harper Collins, New York, USA. 2013.

Veggeberg, Scott. *Medication of the Mind.* Henry Holt & Co., New York, USA. 1996.

Wagner, C. Peter. *Confronting the Powers.* Regal Books, Ventura, CA, USA. 1996.

Wesley, John. *The Journal of the Rev. John Wesley.* (Vol. 1.) J. M. Dent & Sons Ltd, New York, USA. 1906.

West, Morris. *A View from the Ridge.* Harper Collins, Pymble, AUS. 1996.

Whitaker, Robert. *Mad in America: Bad Science, Bad Medicine and the Enduring Mistreatment of the Mentally Ill.* Basic Books, New York, USA. 2001.

Whybrow, Peter. *A Mood Apart.* Harper Collins, New York, USA. 1997.

Winchester, Simon. *The Surgeon of Crowthorne.* Penguin Books, London, UK. 1998.

Zwar, Desmond. *Doctor Azzhead of His Time: The Life of Psychiatrist Dr Ainslie Meares.* Greenhouse Publications, Richmond, AUS. 1985.

Zweig, Connie and Wolp, Steve. *Romancing the Shadow.* Harper Collins, New York, USA. 1997.

Lightning Source UK Ltd.
Milton Keynes UK
UKOW05f2037060417
298531UK00001B/42/P